The FRIGHTFUL AND *Joyous* JOURNEY OF FAMILY LIFE

The FRIGHTFUL AND *Joyous* JOURNEY OF FAMILY LIFE

H. WALLACE GODDARD

BOOKCRAFT
Salt Lake City, Utah

Library of Congress Catalog Card Number: 97-71359
ISBN 1-57008-318-5

First Printing, 1997

Printed in the United States of America

For Nancy,
Emily, Andy, and Sara,
who have given me so much family joy!

For parents and ancestors
whose noble examples
have taught us to seek
joy.

And
for Heavenly Father,
who makes it all
joyously possible.

For to miss the joy
is to miss all.

—*Robert Louis Stevenson*

CONTENTS

ACKNOWLEDGMENTS

Jeff Hill persuaded me to undertake this book project. He, Brent Miller, Mark Kunkel, and Julie Bullen gave valuable feedback on drafts of the work. George Durrant provided encouragement and helped me connect with a publisher. And Cory Maxwell provided the patience and encouragement to complete the project. Thanks to these people and the many friends who have taught me so much with their lives.

PREFACE

Heavenly Father has perfectly designed family life to make us crazy, or to help us grow.

One day the phone interrupted my wife's and my quiet lunch. The woman on the other end of the line was desperate. "Come immediately!" she demanded. I stammered. That is not the way people usually invite us over for a visit. The mother repeated: "Come immediately. I think I'm going to kill my daughter."

Nancy and I jumped into our car and drove to the house. When we arrived, we were met at the door by the tense mother. The four-year-old daughter cowered in the corner. As the mother told us the story of her girl's misdeeds, we worked our way to the sofa.

"I cannot believe her! She has been playing with the dog. Several times today she got the dog in the corner and kicked it! Can you believe that? She doesn't care about the dog's feelings!" The mother continued to itemize the little girl's offenses. "She leaves the hall light on during the day, even though I've told her to turn it off! She brings cookies into the living room." The mother was at her wit's end.

Because we had tended the girl many times, we knew her well. She seemed to be a normal four-year-old: sometimes care-less and childish, but not vicious.

As we talked with the mother, the child became more relaxed and began again to play with the dog. She was sitting on the floor in front of us when she aggressively pulled the dog toward her. The mother launched herself from the sofa, ran to her daughter, kicked her, and turned to us to pronounce: "See! She does not care about the dog's feelings!"

The irony would have been comical if it had not been tragic: The mom was angry that her girl was cruel to the dog, so the mom was cruel to the daughter. Perhaps this little girl was the scapegoat for her mom's exhaustion, frustration, and loneliness. Perhaps the mom was a hostage in her own unhappy life and a four-year-old was her prisoner. Both were miserable.

Nancy and I volunteered to take the girl for a few hours—or a few days—while the mom had a chance to relax and sort out her feelings. Sometimes we are cruel in families because it is all we know. Sometimes we are cruel because there is so much unhappiness pent up inside of us. Sometimes we are cruel because we think there is no alternative or because we think it is effective in teaching children.

A lot of things are like that. "There's always an easy solution to every human problem—neat, plausible and wrong" (H. L. Mencken, quoted in Laurence J. Peter, comp., *Peter's Quotations* [New York: William Morrow and Co., 1977], p. 428). The decision to be miserable is one of those solutions to an imperfect world. It is neat, plausible, . . . and wrong.

The gospel has always taught us that things are not as we expect: To grow up, we must become childlike. To find ourselves, we must lose ourselves. The poor will be rich. The last will be first.

So the truth about family principles is often a surprise. Sometimes things are the opposite of what we expect. One of the great unexpected truths may be that we can experience joy even in the most trying circumstances.

But for family life to be joyous requires more than good intentions. It requires the application of true principles. It also requires that we bring our best efforts and our warmest affection to the task. In addition, we must get heavenly help.

The parent who is determined to have a storybook family may have made the fundamental mistake of assuming that the process is about happy partnerships and satisfying childrearing. The process is about growth. And growth does not come without pain and mistakes. There may be no situation in which we make more mistakes than in family life. And there may be no situation in which we learn more than in the covenants and struggles of family living. The family is where our understanding of gospel principles is tested and refined.

So, with all the challenges, is family joy possible? The answer keeps surprising us. Joy is possible *because* of the struggle. Consider the themes of Lehi's great final Atonement address: "For it must needs be, that there is an opposition in all things. If not so . . . righteousness could not be brought to pass, neither wickedness, neither holiness nor misery, neither good nor bad. . . . But behold, all things have been done in the wisdom of him who knoweth all things. Adam fell that men might be; and men are, that they might have joy." (2 Nephi 2:11, 24, 25.)

Joy is not the fruit of a tranquil life. Joy is the sure marker of Heavenly Father's presence, care, and redemptive purpose. That presence is sought and appreciated most in times of difficulty and adversity. With the Father's joy-bearing presence, the struggle is meaningful and survival is possible.

This book is an attempt to share years of study and years of mistakes with others who are in this same frightful and joyous journey of family life. There are some things I know most certainly about this journey: Our growing is supervised by a Father who is good, loving, and brilliant. He also is committed to blessing us. He is able to do his work even when we cannot understand his purposes. Family life is perfectly suited to teach us, stretch us, and bring us joy.

The Lord counsels us to seek learning by study and by faith (see D&C 88:118; 109:7; 109:14). By applying wise principles and divine inspiration, we can make the challenging journey with more hope and more joy and with fewer mistakes. I continue to be amazed at the goodness and ingenuity of Heavenly Father's plan. I say with Nephi: "O how great the plan of our God!" (2 Nephi 9:13.)

One

BLOCKAGES TO JOY

And that wicked one cometh and taketh away light and truth.
—D&C 93:39

"Housing officials in Spokane, Wash., Tuesday gave cleanup deadlines to Kathleen Henry, whose house is so filthy it has sickened garbage workers. The city plans to demolish the home if she misses the deadlines. Officials say there are animal feces on floors and garbage stacked to the ceilings. Two trash collectors became ill March 17, so firefighters with respirators finished the job." (*USA Today*, 30 March 1995.)

It is hard to imagine a house so filled with trash. Imagine the odor! Imagine the challenge of navigating between piles of garbage! Imagine sitting for a meal! Such a pile of trash would take over family life and intrude on every activity.

The same may be true in our lives when we let emotional, social, and spiritual debris accumulate. In one corner of our hearts is resentment for people who have neglected us. In the middle of the floor is hostility for people who have cheated us, judged us, or hurt us. The piles of stinking garbage can pile up and make it impossible to conduct normal life without tripping on the piles or choking on the foul odor. Such a mess makes the prospect of joy very remote. Reflect on your emotional life. What are some of the things that block your joy? Are there heaps of resentments, fears, inadequacies, anger, grudges, or guilt that stack up in your life? Reflect on the last hours, days, and weeks. What are the thoughts and feelings you bump into that block your personal experience of joy?

Each of us has characteristic strengths. We also have characteristic weaknesses. Satan has watched us for decades. He knows what damning behaviors have stopped us in the past. He knows what is likely to work again.

How do we deal with the piles of stinking garbage that accumulate? The world's way of dealing with the problem is to ask where all this stuff is coming from. "A full-scale investigation is needed," we say. We study the source, nature, and accumulation of garbage. We can become quite obsessed with our study of garbage.

But the Lord's way is different. We know because of our eternal perspective that trash is pretty normal in a telestial world. We also know that we ought not to study trash. The Savior comes to our door as the cheerful and capable sanitation engineer. He says: "I'd sure be glad to haul off all that trash. May I?" Surprisingly, many of us do not allow him to do what he is uniquely able and completely willing to do. Why do we resist his offer?

Sometimes we are too embarrassed to let him see our trash. We try to hide our mistakes because of our shame. But how can we hide anything from him? For example, a beautiful friend told us of her youthful errors, her feelings of guilt, and her continuing sense that Christ wanted to come and wash her feet and cleanse her soul. But she was horrified by the thought. How could she let the Master of the world near her when she was so impure? Yet, his conversation with each of us is as it was with Peter: "Peter saith unto him, Thou shalt never wash my feet. Jesus answered him, If I wash thee not, thou hast no part with me." (John 13:8.)

We will never be clean without his help. Every activity may be judged by the way it draws us closer to Christ or further from him. When you feel him knocking at your door, are there thoughts or doubts that keep you from letting him in?

Not only sin but also excessive self-sufficiency can keep us from drawing close to him. "I must clean up my house before I could allow him to see it," some say. It is ironic that we would try to clean our houses without the help of the great Sanctifier. We should be alert to any attitude or thought that keeps us from welcoming him when he knocks at our door.

Sometimes we will not let him help us because we do not trust him. I learned a valuable lesson about trusting him from a member of our branch who came to see me as a friend because she was not willing to see me as her branch president. Her life was filled with problems, doubt, sin, and confusion. She asked me what she should do. I suggested that she let the Savior in to help her make sense of her life. She resisted. "If I let the Savior into my life," she said, "he will tell me all the stuff I am doing wrong. He will start to make a bunch of demands and insist that I entirely clean up the place. I don't need that kind of help." A suggestion came to mind. I suggested that the next time she felt him knocking at her door, she open the door of her life to him. But tell him that he can come in only to the linen closet of her life and he can stay for only ten minutes. Then he must leave without resistance. She was aghast at the presumption. But, with encouragement, she resolved to try. The same woman returned to my office a week later, subdued and peaceful. She closed the door and sat down. "I invited him in and told him he could stay only for a few minutes," she said. She paused for a long time. "I have never known such joy. He taught me. He loved me. He encouraged me. Why didn't anyone ever tell me that the Savior was like that?"

Perhaps his goodness is the best-kept secret in the world. Because of him we have nothing to fear. We are infinitely better off in his hands than in Satan's or even our own. "Come unto me, all ye that labour and are heavy laden, and I will give you rest" (Matthew 11:28) is his invitation.

Joy can also be blocked by fear. I think of a dear friend who called me when he was wrestling with a difficult career decision. He worried that he was not in tune with the Spirit. He feared that the Lord would not guide him because he had disappointed the Lord many times over the previous twenty years. He doubted his worthiness and ability to receive inspiration. He feared that he would make a bad decision and ruin his family and professional life. Who among us has not worried about a decision, our worthiness for inspiration, and the pureness of our answers? He asked my advice. Two suggestions sprang to mind. Because the suggestions are wiser than any I could think of, I felt certain that Father was directing. First, cast out doubt and fear. Recognize that uncertainty, misery, and doubt (especially self-doubt) are from the devil. Cataloging previous errors does not help us make the current decision. Get rid of all negative thoughts and feelings. In the words of President Howard W. Hunter, "Don't take counsel from your fears" (as quoted in Robert D. Hales, "A Testimony of Prophets," in *BYU 1993–94 Devotional and Fireside Speeches* [Provo, Utah: University Publications, 1994], p. 162). Second, find a quiet place. Take time for peaceful meditation. Consider the options. Preview the opportunities and challenges that each option offers. Then, without defenses, excuses, or worries, sense which course offers the greater joy. Don't let your worries block the answers that are in your spirit. That eternal spirit knows what is right for you. Simply follow the path of joy. It leads to peace. It leads to growth. It leads to the Father.

A close cousin to fear is anxiety. Anxiety can be mild and occasional, or it can be common and disabling. John said, "There is no fear in love; but perfect love casteth out fear" (1 John 4:18). Anxiety may be the perfect fear that casts out love. A good friend confided in us her constant, nagging fear that her toddler son would get past their fence, fall in the stream, and drown. She was tormented every day by her anxiety for her son.

Is such anxiety a message from our Father? Is he inspiring her misery as a warning? I don't think so. I think Satan is holding her hostage. We suggested she seek counsel from Heavenly Father. He may direct her to better secure the bottom of the fence or to instruct the brothers to keep an eye on the little one. He may direct her one day to go directly to the stream if her son is in danger. Or he may counsel the family to move. But Heavenly Father does not nag.

Sometimes we miss joy because we don't think about it. We forget what is most important to us. I remember when our son Andy was small, maybe three or four years old. He used to like to sleep in odd places, such as the linen closet or an empty bathtub. One night he asked if he could sleep on the floor in his sister's room. After we consulted with Emily, it was agreed that he would spread his sleeping bag on the floor in front of her old dresser. In the wee hours of the morning, I was awakened from a sound sleep by a muffled cry. Somehow I knew instinctively what had happened. I knew that the old dresser with a bad leg had somehow had the supporting can of paint knocked out from under it and that the dresser had fallen over on our sleeping son. I found myself launched from my bed and unbidden words escaping from the deepest part of my soul: "No! Not my Andy!" I ran to the bedroom and found the heavy dresser covering my son. I immediately pulled it off him and dragged it into the hall. Then I comforted Andy. Fortunately he was not badly hurt. After some loving, he returned to sleep. I promptly found a saw and cut off the other three legs to match the broken one so that the dresser would never fall over again on a beloved child.

I was never the same after that experience with Andy. It helped me remember what I already knew: that Andy, Emily, and Sara mean more to me than life itself. Plato said that all learning is remembering. And God gives us many reminders lest we forget what things matter most: the things of eternity, the people who are our eternal companions.

Hate, judgment, and resentment are especially effective at blocking joy. They take enormous amounts of room in our souls! Sometimes we try to convince ourselves that our hostility is some kind of righteous indignation as we process our injuries and other people's errors. But the person who will not forgive carries an unbearable burden. In him or her remains the greater sin (see D&C 64:9).

Frederick Buechner writes: "Of the seven deadly sins, anger is possibly the most fun. To lick your wounds, to smack your lips over grievances long past, to roll over your tongue the prospect of bitter confrontations still to come, to savor to the last toothsome morsel both the pain you are given and the pain you are giving back—in many ways it is a feast fit for a king. The chief drawback is that what you are wolfing down is yourself. The skeleton at the feast is you." (*Wishful Thinking* [San Francisco: Harper San Francisco, 1973], p. 2.) Buechner is right. Anger consumes us.

Months ago I read of a woman who was murdered. The story told of the family's tenacious search for the killer. Through years of determined investigation they finally tracked down the killer and brought him to justice. The story concluded by saying that now, at last, the family could be at peace. At peace? I believe that criminals do need to be apprehended, and they need to account for their behavior, and society needs to be protected from those who have no conscience. But how does this story fit with your experience? When you crowd an offender into a corner and prove his or her guilt, do you feel better? My experience is that usually my accusations lead to counter-accusations, and my enemy and I both feel increasingly indignant, angry, and misunderstood. The search for justice spirals down into the boiling lava of hatred and recrimination. We become addicted to our cruel crusade. Any sense of triumph has the hollow and short-lived feel of Cain's glorying after the murder of his brother: "I am free." (Moses 5:33.)

In some sense, Cain was free; free as a fugitive and a vagabond. The natural man, unchanged by the Spirit of God, experiences lots of such self-deceiving nobility and empty victories. Does one feel better after getting revenge? Can there ever be enough revenge? Does wrestling a foe into submission bring peace? Or are hate and envy addictive? Does Satan laugh when he gets us swept up in battering other people with our rightness?

I have felt the powerful lure of such passions. At one time in my life I felt desperately hurt and betrayed. I was tempted to be bitter, to blame my tormentors, and to excuse my own behavior. As I filled my spare time with weeding the garden in our backyard, I felt resentment start to fill my thoughts. "It isn't fair!" I protested. But the bitter temptation had an ugly face. I knew that my survival depended on keeping my soul from filling with such bitter dregs. I knew I had to keep the ugliness out. So I sang hymns. I told myself jokes. If anyone had seen me in the garden singing, laughing, and weeping, they might have thought me crazy. But I knew that I must not surrender to ugliness.

Maybe we are like fish who discover water last. Immersed in the divine element, we never notice it, never marvel in it, never use it. Thomas Clayton Wolfe said something similar but in stronger words: "Poor, dismal, ugly, sterile, shabby little man . . . with your scrabble of harsh oaths . . . Joy, glory, and magnificence were here for you . . . but you scrabbled along . . . rattling a few stale words . . . and would have none of them." (Quoted in Laurence J. Peter, *Peter's Quotations* [New York: William Morrow and Co., 1977], p. 6; ellipses in original.)

For each of us, joy may come easily and naturally or it may come reluctantly and hesitantly. But maybe we all live beneath our potential for joy.

Again, inventory your emotional life. Are there things that interrupt our joy? Do we cherish our trash? Are there thoughts and feelings that keep us from letting the Lord haul off the trash in our lives? We do not need to cling to trash. We can let him haul it off so that we can discover joy. Our telestial natures may resist, but we can learn the processes of joy.

Two

SURPRISED BY JOY

Adam fell that men might be; and men are,
that they might have joy.
—2 Nephi 2:25

So what is joy? Is it the promised state of those who righteously endure in this life? Is it an ultimate compensation? Is it the final reward for having a well-developed capacity for suffering? Joy may be all of that, but it is more. It is the consuming sense of God's presence, goodness, and love. It is an indescribable sense of meaning.

C. S. Lewis, in his autobiography, tells of being surprised by joy. He tells of standing as a youth on a summer day remembering his brother's toy garden. "It is difficult to find words strong enough for the sensation which came over me; Milton's 'enormous bliss' of Eden comes somewhere near it." Describing other experiences of joy, he says, "I desired with almost sickening intensity something never to be described. . . . I call it Joy. . . . [A]nyone who has experienced it will want it again." (*Surprised by Joy: The Shape of My Early Life* [New York: Harcourt-Brace Jovanovich, 1956], pp. 16–18.)

Why should the recollection of a childhood experience inspire joy? Does it have any spiritual significance? That, perhaps, is the surprise. Joy comes unexpectedly. It is as likely to come from a walk in a garden as from reading a great book of theology.

The scriptures tell us that the Lord "comprehendeth all things, and all things are before him, and all things are round about him; and he is above all things, and in all things, and is through all things, and is round about all things; and all things are by him, and of him, even God, forever and ever" (D&C 88:41). In all of creation, he is there. It is hard to know when the remarkable sense of divinity will descend upon us. "The wind bloweth where it listeth" (John 3:8). But when joy fills us, we should notice and be grateful.

Joseph Smith described the way joy can increasingly fill our life experience as we progress. "The nearer a man approaches perfection, the clearer are his views, and the greater his enjoyments, till he has overcome the evils of his life and lost every desire for sin" (*Teachings of the Prophet Joseph Smith*, comp. Joseph Fielding Smith [Salt Lake City: Deseret Book Co., 1977], p. 51).

Joy is the natural result of being connected with the Divine. Fortunately it operates on a spiritual economy in which abundance rather than shortage is the natural state. In fact, joy is contagious. Just seeing your experience of joy can fill me with joy.

In the experience of joy, as in other experiences, we may live far beneath our potential. At times we may not even seek joy because we do not expect to find it. Why don't we experience more joy? Part of the reason may be that we are confused about the source.

Satan, the great deceiver, the father of lies, has cast himself as a fun friend; a party animal; a jolly, fun-loving, gracious sort of guy. And he has cast God as Scrooge, a closefisted, scrimping, exacting taskmaster. According to one author's portrayal, Satan teaches that God is "the sort of person who is always snooping round to see if anyone is enjoying himself and then trying to stop it" (C. S. Lewis, *Mere Christianity* [New York: Macmillan Pub. Co., 1943, 1945, 1952], p. 69).

What a fiendish inversion! It is a perfect lie! When we expect fun with Satan and only chiding and misery from the Father, we are not likely to turn to the Source of joy.

Nothing could be further from the truth. Satan wants all people to be miserable, just as he is. So he promises fun, freedom, and happiness at an exorbitant price. Then he delivers hurt, disappointment, cynicism, empty sorrow, broken contracts, broken lives, and profound and lasting pain.

Heavenly Father is just the opposite. Infinitely loving, he arranged to satisfy the demands of justice with the willing, eternal sacrifice of his son so that he can bring his imperfect but earnest children home, justified, sanctified, and taught. His work and glory are to help us attain an eternal joy. He is dedicated to nothing but blessing his children both in the eternal worlds and along the way.

What a father! What a friend! What a redeemer!

So, if he is so gracious, what is it that keeps us from joy? What can we do to experience more joy in our lives?

The first key in experiencing joy is to cast out all evil. The accumulation of garbage mentioned in chapter one illustrates the idea. One more gruesome metaphor might be useful.

Imagine being awakened in the night by convulsions in your stomach. Having earlier sensed some symptoms of the flu, you had prepared yourself with a pan by your bedside. As the waves of nausea rack your body, you empty your stomach into the pan. With your stomach emptied, you feel some relief. What do you do with the malodorous contents of the pan? Would you save the pan and its contents? Would you keep them at your bedside for months, occasionally uncovering the pan to fill your nostrils with the offensive odor?

The idea is monstrous! It is hard to imagine anyone saving such a putrid mess. But maybe many of us do something similar to that. Sometimes we save our pain, our anger, our imperfections, and our mistakes.

Have you ever been deeply hurt by the thoughtlessness of a friend or family member? Have you found yourself dwelling on the hurt, mulling over in your mind the injustice and meanness of the perpetrator? Have you found, as I have, that the anger becomes obsessive? Soon we can think of nothing but the injustice. Anger and indignation fill up our souls. They leave no room for peace, joy, or love.

Have you ever done something foolish, silly, or cruel and found yourself flailing yourself for your mistake for weeks or months? Perhaps the unpleasant memory haunts your quiet moments?

If we are to become efficient in joy, maybe we need to be good at recognizing when evil is troubling our souls. We should not fret about it. Merely notice it and turn away from it.

Even remarkable Nephi must have felt deeply troubled when he proclaimed: "Nevertheless, notwithstanding the great goodness of the Lord, in showing me his great and marvelous works, my heart exclaimeth: O wretched man that I am! Yea, my heart sorroweth because of my flesh; my soul grieveth because of mine iniquities. I am encompassed about, because of the temptations and the sins which do so easily beset me. And when I desire to rejoice, my heart groaneth because of my sins." (2 Nephi 4: 17–19.)

Nephi's heart groaned because of his sins! That is a surprise! Maybe we are not alone in sensing the cruel inroads of evil into our minds and hearts.

Is it possible to bring joy, peace, hope, purpose, and love to a life that is such a mess? The Lord seems to think so. He modestly assures us that he is able to do his work (see 2 Nephi 27:20–21). His work is blessing and teaching his children.

The process starts with disposing of the trash. For each of us the misery traps may be different. For one person it is the fearful unwillingness to accept imperfection in himself or herself together with the compulsive need to blame others. For another person the trap may be the chronic blaming of self. For another person it may be fear.

The scriptures say, "And finally, I cannot tell you all the things whereby ye may commit sin; for there are divers ways and means, even so many that I cannot number them" (Mosiah 4:29). It seems that many of the most popular sins of the latter days are sins of feelings. That is not surprising given that Satan wants to keep us confused and unable to access or process the subtle impressions that come from the still, small voice.

How can we discover our personal traps? Moroni gives us a test that is simple and direct. "For behold, the Spirit of Christ is given to every man, that he may know good from evil; wherefore, I show unto you the way to judge; for every thing which inviteth to do good, and to persuade to believe in Christ, is sent forth by the power and gift of Christ; wherefore ye may know with a perfect knowledge it is of God" (Moroni 7:16). We may know what is good because it leads us to Christ.

On the other hand, "Whatsoever thing persuadeth men to

do evil, and believe not in Christ, and deny him, and serve not God, then ye may know with a perfect knowledge it is of the devil; for after this manner doth the devil work, for he persuadeth no man to do good, no, not one; neither do his angels; neither do they who subject themselves unto him" (Moroni 7:17). Anything that does not lead us to Christ is evil. This is a bold doctrine. But it is sensible. Joy comes from a healthy relationship with Christ. Evil comes from turning from his power. The Book of Mormon teaches this idea clearly: "For I say unto you that whatsoever is good cometh from God, and whatsoever is evil cometh from the devil" (Alma 5:40; see also Omni 25; Ether 4:12; and Moroni 7:12, 24).

Applying this principle in our lives takes some discernment. As we examine our lives, we may consider: Which of my daily activities leads me to Christ, to his kind of growing, loving, and serving? Which of my daily activities draws me into behavior incompatible with his divine companionship? Some behaviors are obviously out of bounds: cruelty, pornography, stealing, cheating, and so on. But there are other inappropriate behaviors that are surprising. One may find that the study of some worldly philosophies makes one cynical, seeing only the bad and weak in humans. Hanging out with certain friends may lead to sarcasm. Excessive shopping can make us vain. Listening to mocking voices can make us arrogant. Thinking we need to suffer before we go to the Father for healing balm when we have sinned can keep us from needed heavenly ministrations. What are some activities that lead you from Christ or keep you from him?

What are some of the things that block your joy? Forgetting? Fear? Hate? Guilt because you are not better than you are? Dismay that you are not like someone else? Resentment or anger? Since all ugliness comes from the father of lies, see if you can discern the falsehoods that block your connection with Heavenly Father. Some of them may be disguised as righteousness. For example, sometimes we imagine that self-hatred is good. But it is a poor substitute for humility, which is the deep sense of our need for God. Can you see places where you follow the subtle voice of Satan?

A second step in filling ourselves with joy is to have hope. Recently I returned from work to find a note from my wife. She wrote: "Sister so-and-so called and asked me to ask you, 'Is it reasonable to be unhappy?'" What a poignant question! The dear sister who asked the question is a new member in our ward who is struggling with many family demands, working valiantly, but feeling miserable.

Is it reasonable to be unhappy? Probably. In fact, in a telestial world it is normal. But under most circumstances it is not necessary.

There are as many different causes for misery as there are different physical ailments. There is no one medicine that will cure all ills. But there is one Physician who can prescribe the cure. He knows what medicine will cure each malady.

The Lord taught us the general processes for healing: forgive, love, serve. The same familiar processes apply both for cleaning out our souls and for perfecting ourselves. We may have hope for a cure because of his capable care.

Nephi modeled wise behavior. Right after the previously-quoted cry of despair, he exclaims: "Nevertheless, I know in whom I have trusted" (2 Nephi 4:19). That is the turning point: Nephi's reliance on Christ! He adds:

> And why should I yield to sin, because of my flesh? Yea, why should I give way to temptations, that the evil one have place in my heart to destroy my peace and afflict my soul? Why am I angry because of mine enemy?
>
> Awake, my soul! No longer droop in sin. Rejoice, O my heart, and give place no more for the enemy of my soul. . . .
>
> O Lord, wilt thou redeem my soul? Wilt thou deliver me out of the hands of mine enemies? Wilt thou make me that I may shake at the appearance of sin? . . .
>
> O Lord, wilt thou encircle me around in the robe of thy righteousness! O Lord, wilt thou make a way for mine escape before mine enemies! Wilt thou make my path straight before me! Wilt thou not place a stumbling block in my way—but that thou wouldst clear my way before me, and hedge not up my way, but the ways of mine enemy. (2 Nephi 4:27–28, 31, 33.)

Nephi's psalm provides an eloquent and powerful testimony of our reliance on Christ. Only he can haul off the trash that litters our souls. We are wise not to accumulate or dwell on anything evil. If we are to be clean, we must get his help in hauling off the stored misery and purging ourselves of the effects of our inevitable soiling by telestial experience.

There is a third step in filling our lives with joy. If we imagine again our psychological and spiritual lives to be like houses, then it is clear that it is not enough to haul off the garbage. A clean but empty house is not a fitting home. We must let in sunlight and bring in fresh water, nourishing food, comfortable furnishings, and helpful friends. We must fill our homes with purposeful growing and serving.

Sometimes it is difficult for us to discover our individual missions. Most of us consider ourselves to be quite unremarkable people with no particular gifts or purposes. We may see ourselves as merely crowd-swellers in the drama of life. Yet (notice if the Spirit affirms this for you) it seems that the Lord has a special mission for each of us. He has unique gifts for each of us to use in our service. He has designated places where he would have us bless, comfort, and teach. The Spirit insists to me that this is true. The ways he calls on us to serve may be surprisingly modest, but they are the sure path to joy.

How do we find our individual missions? I think that one of the most effective ways is to discover what we love. After all, our spirits come from God filled with a half-eternity of growing and learning. As we discover the things that we love, we may know what our spirit is uniquely prepared to do.

Barbara Sher has recommended that each of us list twenty things we love to do (see *Wishcraft: How to Get What You Really Want* [New York: Viking Press, 1979], p. 46). Can you do that? Can you dig into your heart and find twenty things that you love? Maybe you love to sing hymns as you work around the house. Maybe you love to look at magazines that show beauty in the world. Maybe you love to read. Maybe you love flowers. Maybe you love to garden. See if you can list twenty things you love to do.

Noticing the things that we love to do can teach us much about our unique gifts and missions. There are additional, practical reasons to list what we love. One is that we may discover that we are already doing many things that we love. It is important to be aware of them. We may find that our lives are filled with abundant small pleasures, such as being with our children, learning, being busy, helping people. Each of us should celebrate the good things that are already in our lives.

But there is another practical reason to list the things we love. We may be neglecting some very important things in our lives. We may have let some of our greatest joys get crowded out by tiresome obligations. It is important to make room for our joys.

Should we let the pursuit of joy replace our fulfillment of duty? Such an either-or question is not likely to yield a meaningful answer. If, for example, we love to sing, that does not mean that we should stay home from church and sing. Maybe we should sing jubilantly at church, take part in the ward choir and special numbers, and sing around the house.

We may worry that we do not have the time or money to take on other activities. But being aware of the things that bring us joy may help us to do what we are doing more efficiently, more joyously. For instance, when we take our children to the library, we might take a minute to check out a book on gardening, astronomy, or some other favorite topic. Maybe we have neglected a satisfying relationship, so we decide to invite that person to walk with us in the morning. Maybe we want more special time with our children. We might use our children's days off from school to go for lunch together. We can use our creativity to make room for the important, joy-bearing activities of our lives.

When I list the things that I love to do, I find that they include sitting peacefully under a tree, enjoying fresh air, testifying of the Lord's goodness, pondering, and learning. These things may also be enjoyed by almost everyone. Listening to my spirit tell me what renews it can lead me to joy.

There is a predictable pattern to our obedience. Nancy tells of feeling that she should reach out to an aged neighbor widow, but her natural reaction was that the reclusive woman would resent any intrusion. Nancy saw the woman walking to the store one day and fearfully offered her a ride. The woman gladly accepted. She bubbled, "I can't believe that anyone would be so kind! Thank you for the ride!" Both of them have been blessed by the relationship that resulted. Obedience to the mandates of our souls brings us joy and blesses those around us. Heavenly

Father is able to arrange things that efficiently! While we are growing and rejoicing, we are blessing other children of his.

As we quietly surrender to Heavenly Father's invitations to serve with our unique gifts, we find that he teaches us more about our gifts, helps us develop them, and helps us bless his other children. Often we violate or ignore the invitation of our conscience because we think we do not have enough time or because we are afraid. But when we do as Father invites, we are unfailingly blessed and often surprised. How is he able to bless us and others at the same time? He is able to do his work!

A fourth step in our search for joy is to notice and be grateful for his gifts of joy to us. "Lift up your hearts and be glad, for I am in your midst, and am your advocate with the Father; and it is his good will to give you the kingdom" (D&C 29:5). Wow! What an encouraging verse! Be glad because he is in our midst, he is our advocate, and he intends to bless us with eternal life! That is good cause for gladness!

Joy is experienced very differently by different people. For me it may come as an emotional flooding of awe for Heavenly Father and his goodness. I cry often and joyously. For one of my dear friends it comes as calm peace accompanied by insight. I suspect that the Father has perfectly tailored our experiences of joy to fit our needs and talents. While it is wise to seek greater joy, I would be foolish to insist that joy come to me in the same way that it comes to you.

Reflect on the places where you see Heavenly Father's kind hand operating in your life. Thank him for them. Rejoice in his goodness. Reflect on the times, places, and activities that bring you peace, joy, and love. Maybe what you feel at those times is an overwhelming sensation that causes you to want to shout from the rooftops. Maybe the feeling is sweet, gentle serenity that leaves you relaxed and peaceful. Maybe a feeling of peace comes when you sing with a choir. Maybe joy comes when you testify. Maybe the feeling comes when you are alone in the woods. Maybe you feel engulfed in love when you serve those in need. List those times that you most clearly feel joy. Notice what they have in common. How can you cultivate experiences of joy?

Joy is not the absence of troubles. It is the sense that our experience has meaning. It is the awareness of the Lord's kind care.

It is the assurance that he will turn our experience to our good. It is a wonderful gift from a perfect Father. It reminds us that he is at home waiting for our joyous return.

I remember a time in my life when I felt very discouraged and worthless. A dear friend named Jack Stone drove many miles and stayed up most of the night to talk with me. He told me a story about his young daughter, who, as her mother's birthday approached, wanted to give her mother a very special gift. But the little girl had no money and very limited, childish skills. So, at her father's prompting, she gathered up the most interesting things she could find, scraps of paper, bits of string, macaroni, watercolors, and glitter. She lovingly glued and painted her treasured finds to a piece of paper and wrapped her gift for her mother. On the appointed day she proudly presented the gift to her mother. What would you guess was the mother's reaction to the gift? Do you think she cringed at the needless waste of macaroni? Do you think she scoffed at the unskilled assembly? No. The mother knelt on the floor in front of her dear child, embraced her, and wept with joy. The mother was touched by the child's sweet message of devotion.

Perhaps it is the same when we make our gifts to Heavenly Father. They are nothing more than shards of good intentions and scraps of struggle. But he is pleased with our earnest effort, and he embraces us in his love.

Picture yourself invited into an office to have an interview with Heavenly Father. What do you think he will say to you? Can you feel him wrapping you in the arms of his love? Picture the blessed interview.

So the starting premise of this book is that joy is available. Joy is not the absence of challenges. It is the awareness that Heavenly Father is helping us, that there is purpose in our struggles, and that he will bless us for our efforts. The journey of life can be filled with joy.

Three

SPECIAL CHALLENGES IN FINDING JOY

*He also gave them strength, that they should suffer no manner
of afflictions, save it were swallowed up in the joy of Christ.
—Alma 31:38*

There are both garden-variety and more exotic blockages to
our joy. Jesus had just returned from the serenity of the Trans-
figuration when he found his disciples stymied by an especially
troublesome demon that had tormented a boy all of his life. The
boy's father besought the Lord for help. The Lord asked that the
boy be brought unto him. The loving father, already disappointed
with the disciples' inability to cure his son, pleaded, "If thou canst
do any thing, have compassion on us, and help us." (See Mark 9:
14–22.)

The Lord instructed the troubled father, "If thou canst believe, all things are possible to him that believeth." The father's
plea must have been inspired: "And straightway the father of the
child cried out, and said with tears, Lord, I believe; help thou
mine unbelief." (Mark 9:23–24.)

We hope. We want to believe. We try to believe. And even
with our imperfect belief, he helps us. He gives us the gift of believing. How often do we cry out in our struggles, "Lord, I believe; help thou mine unbelief."

When Jesus rebuked the evil spirit, the boy fell limp. The
crowd thought him dead. "But Jesus took him by the hand, and
lifted him up; and he arose." (See Mark 9:25–27.) How often do
we appear dead, but he gives us new life?

Later, when Jesus was alone with his disciples, they inquired about their inability to cast out the evil spirit. He taught them that there are some spirits that are especially tenacious. "And he said unto them, This kind can come forth by nothing, but by prayer and fasting." (See Mark 9:28–29.)

One of the most troublesome experiences of my life has been to know earnest, good, committed, wise people who seem unable to find joy or peace. Some of them are tortured by persistent pain and doubt. What is the answer for them? Is hope possible? Why does joy come so readily to some people and so reluctantly to others?

I do not know the answers. But I do believe that the most persistent evil in our lives may not yield to our efforts to remove it because it is hiding in a place we did not expect to find it. For example, we may not feel that we can accept a calling because of our sins, doubts, and inadequacy. Our refusal may seem wise, humble, and honest. We think we are doing what is right, but we are still troubled and haunted. It seems that we can neither accept the call nor reject it. Either way we are miserable.

But Christ can fix all that. He does not promise that it will be instantaneous. Sometimes he requires us to hunt through our mistaken ideas and needless resistance in order to discover the way. More persistent demons may require lengthier, more wise and determined efforts to exorcize them.

In some ways the Latter-day Saint culture is uniquely suited to generate anxiety and depression. We aim at perfection in everything from sewing to parenting, and we are do-it-yourselfers. That is a devastating combination. We will never be able to become perfect if we do not draw on his power. "Learn of me, and listen to my words; walk in the meekness of my Spirit, and you shall have peace in me" (D&C 19:23).

Sometimes it is necessary to involve professionals in the process of pushing the evil out of our lives. Doctors and therapists can sometimes help with depression, schizophrenia, chemical imbalances, and bipolar affective disorder, for example.

One of my heroes is a man named Mark. He is one of the most brilliant and articulate men I know. But that is not why he is my hero. He is honest and earnest and gentle and compassionate. But that is not why he is my hero. Mark confided to me that believing in the gospel is a struggle for him. Sometimes he sees so many inconsistencies. He is troubled by doubts, questions, and frustrations. But he still hopes to make sense of it all.

Mark knows two things that bring peace and joy. One is music. The other is service. So Mark sings and serves and waits for that time when he will not see through the glass darkly. Someday he will see truth face-to-face. That is why he is my hero. He continues to find the little islands of joy in his life, and he tends them with faith and with care.

I am not sure why it should be so hard for Mark to believe when it seems so easy for others. But I honor a person who will be true to that which is fine and noble even without having the peace and assurance that he craves.

Different people have different challenges. I don't know whether they are somehow commensurate with our gifts. But they do seem customized for us. Abraham's life gives us a powerful example of a customized challenge. He learned as a young man to hate human sacrifice as he saw the priests of Pharaoh offer men, women, and children as sacrifices to false gods (see Abraham 1:8). Even his own life was threatened by the wicked priests. The awfulness was intensified by his own dear father's participation in pagan ritual. Yet Abraham, late in life, was asked by God to sacrifice his own cherished son.

Job did not know why he was suffering so terribly. Joseph Smith endured terrible troubles in his short life. Jesus suffered more than any of us. Yet each of them took comfort in doing the best they knew how to do. They endured, and they looked forward to heavenly relief.

I cannot begin to comprehend why some must carry such heavy burdens. A few times in my life the Spirit has been inexplicably and painfully silent. The heavens have been as brass over my head. Without the whisperings of the inner voice, I felt no peace and no hope for finding it. I felt a panic similar to claustrophobia. And I have thought, *I wonder if this is how people feel who have, for example, a chemical imbalance. Trapped. Helpless. What a terrible plight!*

And that is why Mark is a hero. He feels trapped. But he has found those simple, life-affirming activities that bring him joy. He makes them the theme of his life. And he keeps looking for more little islands of joy.

So, for those who cannot seem to find joy, what should they do?

1. Identify those areas of joy God has given you, no matter how small. List them. Music? Art? Serving? Reading? Nature? Friendship? Hobbies? Be alert for any ways that you experience joy and peace. Notice experiences of joy in your life. Enjoy them. Thank Heavenly Father for them! Take comfort in them. Remember them when everything else falls apart.

2. Notice those things that you do that make you feel small and foolish. Notice the traps that keep you from joy. Do you blame yourself for everything that goes wrong? Do you believe that the key to joy is being perfect? Find other ways of interpreting your experiences. Ask advice of wise people whom you trust. Lean on the testimony of those who know. Be patient.

3. Follow the laws of joy. God has recommended some practices as universally beneficial. Decide which of the following practices you can further cultivate as part of your search for joy. Fill your life with them.

Faith: Look for the hand of God in the good things that happen; believe that he is good and loving; look for him in scriptures as well as in your life; believe that God is in control and that your life, despite the pain and confusion, may be right on track with the learning and growth that is just right for you.

Repenting: Clear out old habits; change your ways; seek that which is virtuous, lovely, or praiseworthy.

Serving: Use your talents to help, whether by listening, building, cooking, and so forth.

Enduring: Determine to do all that you can looking for the blessings of a joyous future life; keep serving and trying.

4. Watch for opportunities for more joy. Talk with those who have joy. See if you can discover how they have so much joy. Be warmed by their knowing. If you still find joy and believing to feel unnatural, remember the Lord's statement: "To some it is given by the Holy Ghost to know that Jesus Christ is the Son of

God, and that he was crucified for the sins of the world. To others it is given to believe on their words, that they also might have eternal life if they continue faithful." (D&C 46:13–14.)

5. Get appropriate help. Some people around you may be unaware of your needs, or they may not know how to help. Ask for help. You may also need help from doctors and therapists to discover physical or emotional challenges. Read books by respected authors (see a list of recommended books at the end of this chapter). Study your own life. Look for traps, especially in assumptions or expectations, that may keep you miserable. Be patient. Ask the Lord for insights.

6. Know that you are not alone. While most of us get good at hiding our hurt, pain is real and common. Father, who tracks not only sparrows but every hair of our heads, knows and understands you.

7. Give yourself permission to cry and be totally miserable at times. Notice that heaven may be weeping with you. Endure your struggles the best you can while asking for the Lord's help.

Your unique sensitivity or special challenges may make joy seem hopelessly out of reach. But the Prophet Joseph taught us that joy is the object and design of our existence. We will find it if we persist. (See *Teachings of the Prophet Joseph Smith,* comp. Joseph Fielding Smith [Salt Lake City: Deseret Book Co., 1977], pp. 255–56.) Surely, it will be worth the struggle.

Some books that may be helpful

You may find help from books by capable and sensible scholars, such as the following:

David D. Burns, *The Feeling Good Handbook* (New York: Plume Book, 1990).

Mildred Newman and Bernard Berkowitz, *How to Be Your Own Best Friend* (New York: Random House, 1973).

Martin E. P. Seligman, *Learned Optimism* (New York: Knopf, 1990).

———, *What You Can Change and What You Can't* (New York: Knopf, 1994).

How to Stubbornly Refuse to Make Yourself Miserable about Anything, Yes Anything (New York: Lyle Stuart, 1990).

At times you may want to get a new, more humorous perspective on your challenges. You may choose to read something from cartoon books, or maybe *How to Make Yourself Miserable for the Rest of the Century* (New York: Vintage Books, 1987). Laugh about the silly ways that we make ourselves miserable. Find ways to enjoy your journey through life. Don't expect yourself to be perfect. Enjoy the things you do well. Be patient with your efforts to improve in other areas.

Four

DIVINE GIFTS

To every person is given a gift.
—See D&C 46:11

I remember sitting in a conference on families at Penn State University. One of the presenters asked what we would wish for our children if we could give them anything. I reflected. Several things came to mind. As I pondered, the presenter gave his answer: "If I could give my children anything, it would be high self-esteem."

Instantly it seemed wrong to me. Sure, self-esteem has been the great American cure-all ever since Stanley Coopersmith published his classic work in 1967 titled *Antecedents of Self-Esteem* (San Francisco: W. H. Freeman). We assumed that people with high self-esteem would be happier, kinder, and more productive. But I wondered: What if my son had great self-esteem but he was a gang leader? What if my daughters had great self-esteem but they were cruel or careless people? I also wondered about many of my heroes who appear to have had poor self-esteem. Abraham Lincoln seemed to be filled with self-doubt, but he still served heroically. Enoch saw himself as powerless and unloved. Jesus did not seem to think about himself at all.

In the last few years the community of family scholars and even the popular press have raised serious questions about the usefulness of self-esteem as a predictor of personal functioning. Research suggests that rather than helping people function better, self-esteem comes as a *result* of successes.

The large California study that was to improve the self-esteem of all the state's citizens and show the powerful benefits of self-esteem did something unexpected. It flopped. The project leaders reported that "the news most consistently reported, however, is that the associations between self-esteem and its expected consequences are mixed, insignificant, or absent" (A. M. Mecca, N. J. Smelser, and J. Vasconcellos, *The Social Importance of Self-Esteem* [Berkeley: University of California Press, 1989], p. 15). High self-esteem leads to bad behavior as often as good behavior. Self-esteem is a bust.

There must be something more than self-esteem. Haim Ginott said that there are two qualities we should develop in our children. He said they should become strong and humane. (See Adele Faber and Elaine Mazlish, *Liberated Parents, Liberated Children* [New York: Association Press, 1974].) I say it a little differently: strong and caring. Strong: able to make decisions and face adversity. Caring: valuing people, respecting their feelings, honoring relationships. As long as my children are strong and caring people, I will feel very good about them.

The most important way to develop strong children may be to provide a safe, predictable world where the children regularly experience their own ability to influence the progress of their lives. Discipline is not cruel, unpredictable, or unrelated to their behavior. It is fair, sensible, and oriented toward helping them rather than punishing them.

The most important way to develop caring children may be for them to experience a loving, sensitive, caring environment. Children should know that they are personally valued and respected. More ideas on cultivating these qualities are presented in the chapters on parenting.

Maybe self-esteem has some elements in common with the "strong" part of the formula: respecting self, being capable. But it also borders on self-absorption, egocentrism, and selfishness. The Lord declared: "He that findeth his life shall lose it: and he that loseth his life for my sake shall find it" (Matthew 10:39).

We should have known all along that the traditional self-esteem programs were not the answer. They are contrary to the teachings of the Lord.

The Lord offers something better. It has been available to Latter-day Saints for over 160 years. It is strange that we never thought to consult the Lord about this important matter.

The Lord's program is given in Doctrine and Covenants section 46. It is a revelation on gifts. The revelation clearly focuses on spiritual gifts, but aren't all important gifts spiritual? The Lord's program of gifts does not suffer from the problems that modern self-esteem programs suffer from. As I read that section and the rest of the Doctrine and Covenants, I discovered three major points and two additional supporting points the Lord gives for healthy functioning.

The Lord's first declaration in his program of gifts is: "For there are many gifts, and to every man is given a gift by the Spirit of God" (D&C 46:11). To every person is given a gift. Every person. Not all gifts; a gift. The Lord makes no exceptions. Maybe even the most severely disabled persons have gifts.

One of the great challenges of parenting is helping our children discover their gifts. When you ask most people what their gift is, they will answer, "I don't really have any gifts." In saying that, we may be saying, "I don't really have any important gifts. I wish I were like so-and-so. He or she is so good and so capable. But I keep making the same mistakes. And I am much less than I know I should be."

But the Lord says that each person has a gift. I think that each of us has the gift that is just right for us. Just right. The very one we would pick every time we were given a choice. It is by discovering and using our gifts that we are likely to find the fullest expression of joy.

"For what doth it profit a man if a gift is bestowed upon him, and he receive not the gift? Behold, he rejoices not in that which is given unto him, neither rejoices in him who is the giver of the gift." (D&C 88:33.) Has Heavenly Father given us gifts that we have failed to acknowledge and rejoice in?

There are practical ways we can help ourselves, our children, and others discover personal gifts. In chapter 2 you listed some things that you love to do. The things you love tell a lot about your gifts. Reflect on the activities that bring you joy, the things you love to do. Consider what that tells you about your gifts.

To help young children discover their gifts, we can have them draw pictures or cut out pictures from magazines that illustrate their unique loves. A parent might help each child carve out a unique identity by having a designated place where each child can put up pictures, words, or objects that represent him or her. The adult might occasionally refer to the items, comment on them, and suggest additional good things that characterize that child. This activity is intended to help children discover the positive in their lives. It can help them learn to listen to their own inner voices.

Our loves tell us a lot about our gifts. Our gifts define the unique way Heavenly Father will use us and guide us on our journey back to him.

There are other hints of our gifts. Can you think of experiences or places from your childhood that were magical? I remember making paths through the alfalfa field that bordered our childhood home. I loved exploring and making hideaways in the alfalfa, which was much taller than I was. After the alfalfa was cut and baled, Dad stacked the bales to form a hut. It still warms me to think about those places. I still love the process of exploration and discovery! Reflecting on those cherished experiences has also taught me about the relationships that are most meaningful to me.

Another way to discover your gifts is to play detective. Look around your room, workplace, and home. What are the things you choose to surround yourself with? If you were a detective, what might you conclude about the interests and talents of the person who lives there?

Find something in your house, yard, workplace, or neighborhood that represents you. Do you pick a rock because of your determination or a cloud because of your gentleness or a dirty sock because of your sense of humor? Whatever the object is, what does it say about you?

If you could spend an hour with anyone who ever lived, who would it be? What would you ask? Why did you pick that person? What does it tell you about your interests and gifts that you chose that person?

I have asked hundreds of Alabama teens to identify the person they would spend an hour with. I expected the most common response to be "Michael Jordan." I was wrong. In every gathering where I have asked the question, the most common answer is: "My grandma. I would love to spend an hour with my grandma." Often they tell of having been loved and valued by a grandparent and having that person die when they were children.

They long to be with them again. Maybe this activity tells us less about our distinctive gifts than about our common longing to be connected with the people who gave us life, name, and heritage.

Another way to learn about your soul's gifts is to ask yourself: When was the last time you cried with happiness? What are the things that most often touch your heart? In what kinds of service do you feel most joyous and closest to God?

It is terribly important for each of us to discover the passions and purposes of our individual journeys. Our loves and sensitivities are an excellent guide to those purposes. It is not possible to truly love a bad activity. Love, in its finest spiritual sense, is a holy passion that can lead us to a full expression of our gifts and to our heavenly home.

Some of the above exercises are best done alone. Some of the results can be discussed with trusted friends and family members. Some may be appropriate to do in family home evening. You might have each family member go to his or her own special place in your home or yard and answer those questions that are appropriate. Then have family members regather and share one or two things from their exercises. Support each other's explorations. Reflect to them what you see as their gifts.

The second point in Heavenly Father's program of gifts is: "For all have not every gift" (D&C 46:11). With the exception of those who receive a special dispensation in order to lead the people (see D&C 46:29), no one has every gift. No one.

He calls us to use our personal gifts even though they may seem unimportant. When I was called to be a bishop, I grieved that I was not as wise and dignified as many of the bishops who have blessed my life. I desired Bishop Brown's goodness and Bishop Swain's humility. I tried to be something I was not. I wasn't very good at it. With time I realized that the Lord called me to bring my zeal and zaniness to my service. Of course he also expected me to be wise and balanced, but the Lord can use gifts he has already given me to bless the people I serve.

In a society as competitive as ours, it is natural to never feel good enough. We are flooded with multimedia reminders of the amazing abilities of our heroes. And sometimes we are ungrateful for the seemingly unspectacular gifts God has given us. The wise person asks, "How can I use my gift to bless?" The less-wise person asks, "Why can't I have that gift?"

The fact that our gifts are specific and limited is good news. Since no one has every gift, we all need each other. I need you to share your gifts with me, and you need me to share mine with you. And we both need all the gifts our neighbors offer. It is as Paul said: "For the body is not one member, but many. . . . If the whole body were an eye, where were the hearing? If the whole were hearing, where were the smelling?" (1 Corinthians 12: 14, 17.)

The Lord's message is that every person is different from every other person. And every person is good at something. Maybe a person is strong or gentle or smart or loving or happy or brave. There are many different gifts. Even some things that we see as faults can also be seen as gifts. For example, the person who cries easily may be very sensitive or tender. The person who is stubborn may also be seen as determined or strong. The person who is into everything can also be seen as active and motivated. As you think about each member of your family, consider the positive, unique way each person contributes with his or her unique gift. "But now hath God set the members every one of them in the body, as it hath pleased him. And if they were all one member, where were the body? But now are they many members, yet but one body. And the eye cannot say unto the hand, I have no need of thee: nor again the head to the feet, I have no need of you. Nay, much more those members of the body, which seem to be more feeble, are necessary." (1 Corinthians 12:18–22.)

Even the more feeble make a vital contribution to our families, wards, and neighborhoods. Describe each member of your family (including yourself) in the positive, gift-oriented words that you think the Father might use to describe you.

Your children may become discouraged because of gifts they don't have. One child may want to be athletic, scholarly, and handsome but may be gentle and caring instead. You can help each child value the unique gift he or she is given. Ask them, "If you were to describe yourself as a certain food, what would it be? A doughnut? A chocolate cake? Roast beef? Barbecued pork? A tomato? Lasagna?" Let them tell what food they would choose to be. "How would you feel about having only one kind of food in the world? Why do we need more than one kind of food? Why do we need more than one kind of person? Is it possible that every single person has something special to offer?" As you show your value for each child's gifts, they may come to appreciate and use them more effectively.

Each of us brings unique and appropriate gifts to our life experience. The Lord intends that those gifts be woven into a network of cooperative effort, a network of caring, a network of love—which leads us to the third point in the Lord's program of gifts.

Always remember why the gifts are given: for blessing his children! (See D&C 46:8, 9, 26.) We have gifts so that we may bless each other! "To some is given one, and to some is given another, *that all may be profited thereby*" (D&C 46:12; emphasis added).

If we are to become like the Father, we must learn to bless one another. That is why we were given gifts. Note how the Father uses his gifts: "For behold, this is my work and my glory—to bring to pass the immortality and eternal life of man" (Moses 1:39).

While the devil would have us dread work and service, the Lord suggests that when we use our natural gifts to bless others, it is not disagreeable. It is a joy!

We are more likely to live joyously and productively when we fill our lives with activity and service that is suited to our gifts. What are some of the ways you can use your gifts to serve and bless others? With your unique gifts, what are some service projects you might take on as a person or as a family that are well-suited to your gifts? Is there a member of your family with special challenges who should be allowed to lead the way in a project that features his or her talents? How can you presently use your gifts to help people in your neighborhood? Are there places you would like to volunteer? How can you team your gifts with other people's gifts to accomplish goals that are important to you? Make a plan for projects you would like to complete in your family and community.

Ideally, our life's work gives us many opportunities to use our gifts. Think about the kind of work you would like to do with your life. Close your eyes and plan a normal day that you think would be ideal for you. What do you do when you first get up?

What kind of work do you do? What will your family be like? What do you do with your spare time? In your ideal day, who are some of the people you serve and bless? Family? Neighbors? Community? In your mind, plan out your ideal day.

It was after reflecting on my ideal day some years ago that I realized that my work as a school teacher didn't allow me the opportunities for learning that I craved. So I returned to school so that I could get a PhD. I now have a job that provides numerous welcome opportunities to learn. I love it! Despite the financial setback of years in school, there is no question that it was the right decision for the development of my gifts. If we are to find the work that is right for us, we need to consult our spirits for hopes, dreams, and missions.

There are two supporting points to the Lord's program of gifts. The first is, "Seek ye earnestly the best gifts" (D&C 46:8). We should work to develop those gifts that will make us better able to serve. George Q. Cannon has instructed us in the development of gifts that will make us complete. "If any of us are imperfect, it is our duty to pray for the gift that will make us perfect. Have I imperfections? I am full of them. What is my duty? To pray to God to give me the gifts that will correct these imperfections. . . . God has promised to give strength to correct these things. . . . He wants His Saints to be perfected in the truth." (*Gospel Truth*, sel. Jerreld L. Newquist [Salt Lake City: Deseret Book Co., 1987], p. 155.)

President Cannon described gifts of revelation, wisdom, patience, instruction, a broken heart, and even the gift of governing children. All of these gifts are available to make us perfect in Christ. Note that our perfection is in Christ. During mortality we will never have all gifts but we can be perfect by taking upon ourselves his gifts.

The second supporting point is, "Ye must give thanks unto God in the Spirit for whatsoever blessing ye are blessed with" (D&C 46:32). Failure to acknowledge his goodness is gross ingratitude. He is the gracious giver of all good gifts. Denying or neglecting that God has granted us gifts is not humility; it is ingratitude. The recommended attitude is the acknowledgment that the gifts are literally *gifts*. We can rejoice in the gifts and the giver of the gifts. (See D&C 88:33.)

Parents can do much to help their children appreciate their gifts. "I enjoy your cheerfulness, dear." "I appreciate your gentleness with your pets, son." "You have a very quick and inquiring mind, dear." Such feedback, regularly and wisely given, helps children develop a sense of their gifts.

Sometimes it may not be clear to parents what a child's gifts are. But all children provide valuable clues. What does your child love to do? Read? Talk with friends? Reflect in a quiet place? Listen to music? Draw? The things that children love tell us about the mission that is written in their hearts.

We should give our children opportunities to explore and use their gifts. Emily's room is set up for sewing, Andy's for art, Sara's for reading. It has always been our family policy to underwrite our children's exploration and development of gifts. When Andy wanted to learn to fly, we agreed to provide a trip in a glider (with an instructor) if he would read a book about gliding. He read the book. We provided the ride. As fate would have it, a bad lunch and a bouncy ride dramatically lessened his interest in flying.

To help children understand the way our gifts are woven together, they should hear us admire people for their gifts—admire but not compare. When we compare, it suggests that everyone should be good at the same things. We may admire without comparing. "I love the beautiful way Dawn Hubbard sings." "I enjoy the sincere and richly symbolic stories Mark Kunkel tells." "I admire Aunt Mary's optimism, enthusiasm, and generosity." "I love the way that Nancy reaches out to the lonely." It is easiest to admire and enjoy the gifts that others have when we feel good about the gifts that we have.

"Out of the abundance of the heart the mouth speaketh" (Matthew 12:34). The familiar bucket analogy has some merit. When our buckets are full of joy and purpose, we may be more willing to fill our children's buckets. Paradoxically, the more we pour, the fuller we become.

It is important to give our children opportunities to use their talents in serving others. Spencer W. Kimball often reminded us how vital service is. It connects us with others, and it gives us a taste of the Father's glorious work of blessing his children!

So the Lord has given us a program for understanding and developing our gifts. We will find joy as we use and develop our gifts. His program works beautifully to make us more peaceful and serviceable, more like him.

Many of us have thought that Heavenly Father knew a little about geology and astronomy. Maybe he is also the Master of human development. He has taught us in the scriptures the process to have joy in our gifts and in the Giver of gifts. He knows how to do his work of blessing his children!

Five

CHOOSING A PARTNER

Ye should search diligently in the light of Christ
that ye may know good from evil.
—Moroni 7:19

Marriage commonly provides both joy and misery. A wise choice in our marriage partner makes it likely to have far more joy and less misery in the course of our lives.

There are good reasons and bad reasons to marry a given person. Consider the factors we weigh as we date. Having a nice car confers respectability. Having big plans for the future shows ambition. Being carefree and sociable are valued characteristics.

But apparently it is not easy to make a good choice even after extensive dating; dismaying numbers of relationships end in divorce and heartache. How can a person tell if the nice car really indicates extravagance rather than respectability? Do big plans indicate lack of realism? Is the person carefree to the point of lacking ambition? Is the person sociable or a gadfly? What should a person look for in a partner? Is it possible to make a wise decision?

David and Vera Mace studied and taught marriage enrichment for decades. They recommend three qualities necessary to sustain a relationship. The same qualities are vital in making a marriage decision.

Note: These suggestions are recommended for those who are single. If you are already married, it is not purposeful to plow your relationship history to determine if you have made a mistake. Research clearly shows that couples in stressed marriages often start to reinterpret and rewrite their relationship history. Once we are married, it is wise to ask God to bless and enrich our relationship rather than try to decide if we made a good or bad decision.

The first quality they describe is commitment. Does the person make and keep commitments? There are probably good ways of assessing a person's ability to make and keep commitments. It goes beyond being punctual and never changing majors in school. It probably includes maintaining relationships with family members. Does the person stay in touch with parents, brothers, sisters, and grandparents?

Commitment might also be assessed in the way a person honors moral commitments. Does the person maintain a healthy and continuing relationship with the Church? The person who blames his or her noninvolvement in ward activities on a bad bishop is likely to find problems in another ward. Such attitudes are clear warning signs.

I learned a lot about Nancy's quality of commitment before we even began dating. She and I had gotten acquainted at Church activities. When I ran into her at a college dance, I was delighted. We danced several times. I really enjoyed her. I thought she enjoyed me. As the end of the dance neared, I asked if I could walk her home. She replied, "I would love to walk home with you, but I came to the dance with my roommate. I need to walk home with her."

I was stunned. I didn't expect such an answer. But I was also very impressed. I knew that Nancy was committed. If she was loyal to her roommate, she would also be loyal to her husband. And she has been wonderfully so!

Sometimes we are flattered in relationships when a person likes us enough to dishonor other relationships, break commitments, and even disregard values. That sets a dangerous precedent.

Another quality that the Maces recommend for successful relationships is the creative use of conflict. That may come as a surprise. When we are young, we may expect only token conflict in our relationship. But the wisdom of ages says that differences are inevitable.

President Kimball describes the time when he and Camilla could not agree on a vacation. He wanted to travel, and she wanted to save their money for a new home. They did not come to agreement, so Spencer loaded the car and traveled alone. (See Edward L. Kimball and Andrew E. Kimball, Jr., *Spencer W. Kimball*

[Salt Lake City: Bookcraft, 1977], p. 115.) Even remarkably good people have differences.

But conflicts do not have to be destructive. We may make constructive use of them. My mission president, Glen Rudd, often told us missionaries, "When life hands you a lemon, squeeze it and make lemonade." That is the spirit of creative use of conflict.

When my parents were struggling to raise a family and pay their bills, Mom began to bake at home and sell the goods. For a time she also wrote recipes and articles for the newspaper.

Contrast that with the young woman whose boyfriend dealt with the stress of inadequate money by going out and buying a new Jeep. In my experience, buying a car does not usually generate a lot of capital for the family. Buying a car may lessen the symptoms but it worsens the problem.

When Nancy and I were still getting acquainted, I was impressed by her uncomplaining, pioneer spirit. When, in the course of a water fight in our little rubber raft on the Green River, she fell into a bitterly cold river, I feared that our fun would be ruined for the day. But she did not complain and blame. She climbed back in the raft and continued the water fight. On our first date we were going up a canyon for a hike and picnic. As we entered the canyon on my little motorcycle, it quit and refused to run. I was embarrassed. I proposed several options to get her home or otherwise comfortable. She paused, then said, "No. You sit on the motorcycle and steer. I'll sit behind you facing backwards and push us with my feet." Again, I was amazed by Nancy. I responded, "No. I couldn't let you do that. Why don't you steer, and I will push." Nancy's gentle commitment to help was resolute. We took turns pushing the motorcycle six miles to the shop. Then we went on the picnic. Nancy makes creative use of adversity.

"No man knows his true character until he has run out of gas, purchased something on the installment plan and raised an adolescent" (Mercelene Cox, quoted in Laurence J. Peter, comp., *Peter's Quotations* [New York: William Morrow and Co., 1977], p. 77). It may not be possible to put a potential mate through all those tests before marriage. But it is wise to consider carefully how your would-be partner handles stress and disappointment.

The Maces recommend communication as a third vital quality for successful relationships. Recent research shows us that it is much more than skillfulness in expressing ideas that is important. It is the willingness to use communication to express kindness.

In dating relationships we may think of successful communication as the ability to share deep, personal feelings and have someone take an interest. How many times have we been amazed at the rapt attention new dating partners give to everything the other says. "No kidding! I can't believe it. I hate pickle relish on hot dogs, too! Wow. This is a very special relationship!"

Communication is much more than agreeing on pickle relish. It is more than listening to every word when our relationship is filled with a romantic aura. Good communication has more to do with patience and empathy and finding the good. When two people disagree about how to celebrate Christmas and each person feels that his or her way is the right way, that is when real communication is needed.

Communication includes getting past our feelings and issues so that we can listen with our whole selves in order to understand. Communication is sharing our preferences without making them seem morally superior to our partner's preferences. Good communication takes a lifetime to develop.

So how can you tell if a person will be a good communicator? It is worth noting how the person talks with parents and siblings, especially when they disagree. It is worth noting whether the person will listen for the subtle meanings in the things you say. You should watch for the person's willingness to respect your feelings, listen carefully for your meaning, and look for solutions.

The Maces' three qualities of commitment, creative use of conflict, and communication are vital. But if we waited for someone who was ideal in all three qualities before we married, none of us would marry in this life. When we are together, we can note the quality of relationships the person sustains. It is clear that when we are trying hard to ignore problems and justify our affection, something is wrong.

Before letting the relationship get serious, ask roommates and family members how they feel about the person you are dating. They may be more objective than you are.

The Maces' three qualities are important to look for. But that is just part of the process. There are two other tests: Does being with the person help you be the person you want to be? Does the person help you be peaceful, joyous, kind, and committed? It was clear to me that Nancy was extraordinary in her ability to challenge me to be my best with her unique blend of gentleness and strength. The other test: Does the Spirit of God endorse your choice? My own experience was that the Spirit is not likely to answer a begging, demanding plea, even when accompanied by days of fasting. In the course of our dating I had had sweet affirmations, a sense of rightness in my relationship with Nancy. But when I begged Father for a clear, declarative answer, he seemed to say: "Did I not speak peace to your mind concerning the matter? What greater witness can you have than from God?" (D&C 6:23.) Heavenly Father often gives us the answers as we are carrying on our normal activities of life.

Even in a very good relationship, some things will irritate us. If we are wise, we will notice them and start working on them. Working on them does not mean changing your partner. However, it may mean changing our expectations or behavior. We don't have to wait a decade into our marriage to discover the challenges in our marriages.

Unfortunately, the powerful energies of sexuality are no friend to objectivity. That is why a friendship is the best testing ground for a potential marriage. The more a couple is involved in physical affection, the less likely they are to be objective.

Marriage is a vital decision. It is probably made best when we are not worried about it but when we carry on a healthy friendship. Panic and anxiety do not inspire good decisions. Calm, trusting friendship-building does. The Lord can provide the opportunities that are right for us. We will have opportunities to observe vital qualities in our partners. And the Spirit of God will guide us.

Nephi's brother, Jacob, encourages us to heed inspired counsel so that we "may learn with joy and not with sorrow" (Jacob 4:3). Following sensible and inspired principles in dating and courtship makes us far more likely to be learning with joy.

Six

MARITAL MYTHS

Shouldn't I have all of this and passionate kisses?
—Lucinda Williams
(popularized by Mary-Chapin Carpenter)

"Most couples decide to marry because they love each other and want to spend the rest of their lives together. A man and woman who marry usually hope to share a special sexual relationship and a permanent romantic attraction. But each hopes the other will always be a close friend as well." (*The World Book Encyclopedia,* 22 vols. [Chicago: World Book, Inc., 1993], 13:219.)

A permanent romantic attraction. Interesting idea. It conjures up images of regular dates, flowers, candle-lit dinners, strolls on the beach. A truly American vision of marriage, but maybe not a very realistic or functional one.

Marriage may be made especially difficult by unreasonable expectations, naive hopes, and marital myths. Many of these myths seem sensible enough. Even the most outlandish remain unchallenged because they are hidden in the dark corners of worldly wisdom. Wherever they hide, they can cause immense mischief. They can keep us from experiencing available joy and peace while causing us to search frantically in all the wrong places.

The fundamental marriage myth may be: *I have a perfect right to have my needs met in my marriage.* That is almost like saying, "This marriage exists to meet my needs." That is an eternity away from the Lord's teaching: If you want to find yourself, lose yourself. The myth leaves us always trying to drag affirming behavior out of our marriages. In a telestial world we should not expect to have all our needs met. Maybe when we immerse our-selves in serving in the family, we will truly find ourselves.

A lot of marital dialogue takes the form of, "I wonder if you know how you hurt me or how much I need such-and-such." Sounds like a telestial statement. Telestials ask: "How can I get what I want?" Terrestrials are more likely to ask, "How can we set this up so it is fair? Maybe I can do this for you and you can do that for me." Celestials ask very different questions: "How can I bless you? What can I do to be more helpful, understanding, loving?"

Which questions we ask make a very big difference in our re-lationship. When we ask the wrong questions, we will never get the right answers.

One of the most common marital fictions may be expressed as: "If I can get you to understand what is wrong with you, we will be just fine." In other words, "You need to listen to *me* bet-ter, because I can tell you what is wrong with you and then you can fix it. Then we will be happy."

What a trap! It is filled with forbidden behavior: judging, correcting, selfishness. Sounds much like the familiar mote and beam metaphor that Jesus gave us (see Matthew 7:1–5). Many marriage programs focus almost all of their activity on develop-ing skills for sharing frustrations more effectively. That may be useful at times, but it is not a relationship-building activity, it is a repair activity. And sometimes it is communication in service of devastation. That is not godly. The celestial marriage partner will look for ways to bless.

Another marital myth is, *If I can get you to conform to my image of a good partner, we will be fine.* This myth may be espe-cially pernicious because we have such standardized expectations. The media teach us that a good woman is beautiful, gracious, and composed. A man is brave, strong, and wise. Our Church culture teaches us to expect a woman to be loving, gentle, and filled with charity. A Latter-day Saint man is expected to have a perfect balance of good humor and profound inspiration. Cul-tural expectations can form rigid templates that fit no one and make us unhappy with the best of partners.

I have recently seen a tragic example of this myth in a couple that has been married about thirty years. Both are bright, good people. They have many talented children. But they do not meet each other's definitions of a good spouse. Rather than negotiate their expectations, they have cultivated efficient ways of condemning each other. He hates to be judged or put down and has become hypersensitive to correction. And she likes to correct him. She hates to be treated roughly. And he, impatient with her correction, abuses her verbally. Now, after years of child rearing and occasional closeness, he has reinterpreted their entire relationship history: "It was a mistake. I never should have married her. I never loved her. It was all a terrible mistake."

The devil knows how to design great lies! Even the couple's few great experiences together are lost in the new interpretation. They will stay together until the kids are grown, maybe even until they die. But they treat each other worse than they would treat burglars. They are insulting and cruel. After all, if there is no hope and it all is a mistake, then what can you do but chafe? "I have been cheated. You are not what you ought to be. You have not met my needs." I believe that God holds us accountable for our behavior, for our ungraciousness with each other, and for our harsh and uncompromising expectations.

Our unmet expectations can be a blessing as they teach us about our eternal hopes. They may also teach us about the gaps in our own souls. We may expect a spouse to be attentive and caring because we never felt accepted as a child. We may expect a spouse to be a great spiritual leader because we hunger for divinity that was not satisfied in childhood. Our greatest hopes may be an expression of our greatest pain. We can learn from that.

Consider the ways that you are most often upset with your partner. What can you learn about your expectations? Is it possible for you to make changes that will improve your relationship?

Another myth: *I can help you by reminding you what is wrong with you.* We have good friends whose marriage is probably about normal. Occasionally the husband gets irritated and begins to carp about the wife's faults. She bears it as long as she can. On one occasion she grew weary and reacted, "You know, you have faults too!" And he replied, "Yes. But they don't bother me like yours do!"

How easy it is to be annoyed with our partners when we are weary of fixing our own lives! A familiar maxim comes to mind: "If you don't like someone, the way he holds his spoon will make you furious; if you do like him, he can turn his plate over into your lap and you won't mind" (Irving Becker, quoted in *Pocket Treasury of Great Quotations* [Pleasantville, New York: Reader's Digest, 1975], p. 19).

How tempting it is to try to fix someone else rather than ourselves. It is so much easier! And it is so satisfying to be fixing others. We may even convince ourselves that we are doing something noble. But repenting is something that we do for ourselves, not to others. As we become more Christlike, not only can we better tolerate our partner's lapses but we are likely to draw him or her to greater goodness.

Any irritation with a partner provides a great opportunity to explore our own limitations, expectations, and behavior. Are there chronic issues in your marriage relationship that can help you find areas where you can change? What requests can you make of your partner that may help? What can you do to make the relationship better even if your partner does not change? How can you make your interpretation of your partner more sympathetic and understanding?

When marriages are under stress, it is common for each partner to look for reasons to explain the problems. Looking for reasons may be less productive than looking for solutions. Do you often blame your partner? Do you blame your partner's parents? Are there subtle ways that you judge and accuse your partner even while being polite? Independent of anything your partner chooses to do, what can you do to make your marriage more peaceful and joyous?

The marital dialogue in the movie *The Accidental Tourist* is brilliant:

Sarah: "You know, Macon, the trouble with you is . . ."

Macon: "Sarah, look, don't even start. If that doesn't sum up everything that's wrong with being married: 'Macon, the trouble with you is . . . I know you better than you know yourself, Macon.'"

Sarah: "The trouble with you is you don't believe in people opening up. You think everyone should stay in their own little sealed package."

Macon: "Okay. Let's say that that's true. Let's say for now that you do know what the trouble with me is, that nothing I might feel could suppress, and that the reason I don't want to hear about this specific thing is that I can't open up. If we agree on all that, can we drop it?"

Some things should be dropped, especially the expectation that our partner must change in order for us to be happy.

One of the most tricky assumptions in this myth is the assumption that people are helped to change by being informed of their mistakes. Is that true for you? Are the most important influences in your life people who said to you, "The trouble with you is . . ."? Or has your life been formed and blessed more by people who loved you, thought you were remarkable, cherished you?

Most of us have been motivated to change by confrontation with the painful consequences of sin and our pervasive telestiality. This world provides many such humbling opportunities. But those painful lessons are best orchestrated by God. He has suggested that we stay out of the correcting business and be filled with loving one another. Remarkably, he who has every right to remind us of our shortcomings does so rarely.

There is a myth that seems to be popular among earnest people: *Never go to bed angry.* What? Are you supposed to stay up and fight? There are many marital disagreements that get more caustic and expansive as we discuss them. The assumption that more talking will put the disagreements to rest is probably mistaken, especially when we are tired and angry. It may be useful to agree to save the discussion for later. But wrestling with emotional and divisive issues when we are most tired is not wise.

Some issues should be saved until morning. I am surprised how often my late night indignation is gone by morning! Some issues should never have been brought up at all. They were motivated by selfishness and judgment. Only those that are still an issue when you feel rested, peaceful, and loving need to be discussed.

There is a very subtle myth: *Always be completely honest.* This is tricky territory. Honest sharing can promote openness and intimacy. Honesty is good. But it can also be used cruelly. "I was just being honest when I told her that she isn't attractive anymore." Honesty is not the only value. There is also consideration. When honesty is used to justify the dumping of negative feelings, it is not good. Some things just don't need to be said. The test of any corrective message is: Am I telling this because of my deep desire to bless? We do not have the right to correct anyone we do not love! The Lord commanded us to love with all our hearts. He did not tell us that every grudge and disappointment had to be aired.

This is related to another myth: *In order to deal with a problem, you must get it all out.* Tell your partner how angry you are. He or she needs to know. And you will feel better after you have gotten it out. Think about your experience. Has expressing anger usually helped you calm down? Or, as you express anger, do you often find yourself getting angrier?

For most of us, anger breeds anger. Once we have started to chew out a spouse or child, we feel a need to justify our irritation. Soon it becomes a crusade that engulfs our relationship.

We used to believe that type A aggressive, competitive personalities were more likely to suffer heart disease. But recent research suggests that it is not the activity level but the hostility that kills people. When we interpret people in hostile, cynical ways and express our frustration in hostile ways, we are killing ourselves. (See Redford B. Williams and Virginia Parrott Williams, *Anger Kills: Seventeen Strategies for Controlling the Hostility that Can Harm Your Health* [New York: Times Books, 1993].)

The trickiest myth of all may be, *"I am responsible to make my partner happy."* Some earnest partners (usually wives) accept blame and abuse in a noble effort to be successful in marriage. The trick is that they have defined success in marriage as making the partner happy. Any shortfall is cause for self-blame. Intriguingly, the Lord gives no more endorsement for blame of ourselves than he does for blame of others. We may love and serve. But we cannot guarantee that they will be happy.

This myth is so tricky because some people keep themselves in abusive relationships in a futile effort to please an unpleasant partner. On the other hand, there are those who claim that only their partners are abusive when they themselves are part of an abusive cycle. How does one know if a relationship cannot be saved? A person may seek counsel from Heavenly Father. But sometimes our delicate receptors have been damaged by the hostility. It may be necessary to seek counsel from a trusted friend.

During the time that I served as a bishop, a beloved sister called and asked to see me immediately. When she arrived at the office she told me that she had discovered repeated acts of her husband's dishonesty. She felt that her only choice was to leave him. I encouraged her to consider whether her husband might have some growing still to do. We talked about things she could do to be helpful. When she left, she said something that paid great tribute to her character. "When I discovered my husband's mistakes, I felt that I had to leave him. But I came to you because I knew you would persuade me to do what was right." Her heart told her something different from what her mind had said. Often Heavenly Father expects us to return to difficult situations with the resolve to make them better. Most marriages can be saved by repentance and charity.

The greatest danger of myths may be that they keep us busy at the wrong processes. Our ladder is leaning against the wrong wall. No matter how hard or long we climb, we do not reach our hoped-for joy. But there are better ways: the Lord's ways. "For my thoughts are not your thoughts, neither are your ways my ways, saith the Lord. For as the heavens are higher than the earth, so are my ways higher than your ways, and my thoughts than your thoughts." (Isaiah 55:8–9.)

When we put aside myths, we are likely to find the divine truths about marriage that can help us have a joyous relationship.

Seven

A DIVINE PARTNERSHIP

Neither is the man without the woman,
neither the woman without the man, in the Lord.
—*1 Corinthians 11:11*

Marriage is ordained of God (see D&C 49:15). As Latter-day Saints, we see marriage as a holy blessing. Does that mean that marriage is automatically joyous? No. Most of us have celestial hopes for our marriages, but we have telestial skills. Maybe that is why marriage can be especially stressful for Latter-day Saints. We are working on the delicate task of building a wristwatch with our only tool being a sledgehammer. Our telestial skills are not well suited to the challenges of the delicate celestial task.

We may naively protest when marriage is challenging: "But I have a temple marriage. Why do we have so many problems? It is supposed to be joyous!" Maybe marriage is challenging because it is doing what the Father would have it do: stretch us beyond our telestial habits towards celestial purposes.

When we operate at the telestial level, we ask, "How can I get more pleasure, more fun, more of what I deserve?" We may childishly pout when we do not have the money for a new car or a bigger house or when our spouse does not make us happy. At the terrestrial level we may insist on fairness. "I washed the dishes last night, so you must wash them tonight." Fairness has its place. But fairness is not the highest motivation for marriage. At the celestial level, we ask, "How can I bless and serve?" Celestials know that joy comes in service and growth.

Eugene England has written a brilliant essay entitled "Why the Church Is As True As the Gospel" (in *Why the Church Is As True As the Gospel* [Salt Lake City: Bookcraft, 1986], pp. 1–15). He suggests that the statement "The Church is true" can have several meanings. Commonly we take it to mean that the Church is doing just what it should. It is perfect, give or take an erring member. But the Church can be true in another way. It can be true to God's purposes, true to his intent. And his intent is to help us grow. The stretching and even the disappointment we sometimes feel at church may be true to his perfect design to stretch us to charity.

The same may apply to marriage. It is true to God's purposes. And, true to that purpose, it will provoke growth, often through difficulties. As Elder Neal A. Maxwell has observed, God has compared life to laboring in a vineyard, never to spending a day at a carnival (see "True Believers in Christ," in *1980 Devotional Speeches of the Year* [Provo, Utah: Brigham Young University Press, 1981], p. 136).

So the purpose of marriage is different from what we might have expected. Marriage is intended to draw us up to a full measure of spiritual stature, filled with compassion, charity, and wisdom.

Not only the purposes but also the processes for successful marriage are different from what we might have expected. The Lord has consistently recommended loving and serving as the way to find joy. As a model he has given us the Good Samaritan who, without thought of cost or inconvenience and without judgment or disdain, binds up wounds and cares for the injured. Maybe that general counsel applies also to marriage.

What are the principles of marriage that can help us cultivate a bounteous marital harvest? The first principle of marriage is the same as the first principle of the gospel: faith. While this faith includes trust in our marriage partner, it is more than that. Any faith in a mere mortal will be periodically (perhaps even regularly) disappointed. The heart of wise faith in marriage is the assurance that a loving Father can teach and bless both your partner and you. He can make us into something eternal.

Covenants are a vitally important part of this process. The
Lord uses them continually to help his children. We covenant
with him to do certain things, and he promises to bless us. As we
chafe in a world filled with missqueezed toothpaste, dirty socks,
and cauliflower soup, the Lord points us toward eternal purposes. He promises us "thrones, kingdoms, principalities, and
powers, dominions, all heights and depths . . . and they shall pass
by the angels, and the gods, which are set there, to their exaltation and glory in all things, as hath been sealed upon their heads,
which glory shall be a fulness and a continuation of the seeds forever and ever. Then shall they be gods." (D&C 132:19–20.)

The covenant process is central to what the Lord teaches the
Latter-day Saints in holy temples. In response to our errors and
mistakes, we can go to the Father and make promises to keep
trying and we can ask for his help in doing better.

I recently learned a valuable lesson about covenants. I have
made all the covenants to be a good marriage partner, but I still
find myself being impatient and unkind at times. I recently found
myself inspired to say, "I covenant that, from this time forth, I
will never again be impatient with my sweet partner." Even as I
make such a covenant I know that I am likely to make many mistakes. But I have made it a matter of covenant. I am like the man
who said to the Lord, "Lord, I believe; help thou mine unbelief"
(Mark 9:24). Having made a covenant with Heavenly Father, I
may ask for his incomparable help in keeping the covenant. If I
wait until I have made myself perfectly patient, I will be denying
myself his help. Without his help I will never obtain my objective.

Any number of imperfections in a spouse can be tolerated
when we have a heavenly vision. Some have said, "But I do not
care to spend eternity with that slob I married!" My suspicion is
that if we graciously tolerate each other and struggle to be a little
better, we will be amazed at how attractive our partner is after
the Father has finished working with him or her. So allow a few
faults, and be as Christlike as you know how to be.

"It is a serious thing to live in a society of possible gods and
goddesses, to remember that the dullest and most uninteresting
person you talk to may one day be a creature which, if you saw it
now, you would be strongly tempted to worship. . . . There are
no *ordinary* people. You have never talked to a mere mortal."

(C. S. Lewis, *The Weight of Glory* [New York: Macmillan Co., 1949], pp. 14–15; emphasis in original.) The vision of our eternal possibilities can help us make and keep our covenants.

A good definition of love may be an informed and inspired commitment to share and grow with another person. The commitment should have been informed by examining the relationship during courtship. It can be inspired by a continuing vision of heavenly possibilities.

Robert A. Johnson, author of *We: Understanding the Pyschology of Romantic Love* (San Francisco: Harper & Row, 1983), has said that one of the great threats to lasting marital commitment in our society is the assumption that real love must support a continuing romance (see pp. 99–100). We often refuse to move from the immature view that marriage should be euphoric to the more mature view of partnership, friendship, and acceptance of faults. Many turn to a new relationship rather than giving up their vision of marriage as euphoric romance.

Sometimes we try to sustain romance in marriage with candlelight dinners, evening walks along the beach, or surprise gifts. These things all have their place. But strong couples also enjoy peanut-butter-and-jelly sandwiches while sitting in the backyard. They enjoy working together pulling weeds, painting walls, and washing dishes. Romance alone cannot sustain a continuing relationship. It requires friendship, companionship, and common values.

The successful marriage is filled with many commitments that grow out of our faith in God: commitments to obey him, commitments to be unselfish, commitments to a gospel life, the covenant of fidelity, and a commitment of dedication to God and his purposes.

Faith can make God an active agent in our marital partnership. Our faith in him can cause us to be more patient in our mortal struggles. Our faith in him can help us be more compassionate as a result of reflecting on his great mercy and redemptive commitment. Our faith in him can cause us to ask for that outpouring of grace that will help us overcome our faults and limitations. Faith can be an active power in our marriage relationship when we learn to recognize the negative thoughts about ourselves and our partners and replace them with a vision of the Father's eternal purposes.

Faith is not limited to what happens in our heads. It should lead to many efforts to build and strengthen our relationships in practical ways. When seeing in eternal perspective, a parent can value taking a walk with a son as much as reading the paper, walking a baby in the night as much as sleeping, listening to a struggling child as much as giving brilliant lectures.

Are there ways that we need to affirm our commitments to our marriages? Do I need to set aside time to be with my partner? Do I need to help in additional ways? Do I need to pray for our growth? Do I need to make specific covenants with Heavenly Father to be a better partner?

A second eternal principle that can bless our marriages is repentance. Repentance is the personal willingness to change, improve, and find solutions. It is very different from the common impulse to analyze and blame.

Problems can be destructive. They can generate anger and distance. But they do not have to. They can cause us to be more creative, creative not only in the sense of new solutions but in the sense of being life-giving. Conflict can help us identify areas of needed growth.

But there are traps in the process. It is common for us to respond to conflict by identifying the causes, usually in the character, judgment, and goodness of our partner. And often we become indignant and deliver judging lectures either with strong words or silent rebuffs. But there is a much better way to respond. First, we should ask, "What can I do to solve this problem? Can I be more kind, more helpful, more understanding? Can I learn more about my partner and the situation?" Second, we can make specific requests of our partner rather than complaints. "I would love to spend some time with you. Will you accompany me to the store this evening?" For the process to be creative rather than destructive, both partners must be willing to negotiate, to explore. It may be that your partner hates to go to the store but would be glad to take a walk.

Sometimes we get stuck on blame and anger. We wallow in it, and we do not move toward a solution. Anger can be addictive. Then the more we blame, the angrier we get. Dave Barry has wryly observed that "most married couples, even though they love each other very much in theory, tend to view each other in practice as large teeming flaw colonies" (*Dave Barry Talks Back* [New York: Crown Publishers, Inc., 1991], p. 208).

It is common to either blame our partner or blame ourselves. Neither course is helpful or according to the Lord's plan of happiness. We can respond to problems and differences in more helpful ways. We may choose to look for a solution rather than for blame.

John Gottman is one of the world's leading researchers on marriage. He has categorized marriages into three very different kinds: validating, avoidant, and volatile. He has surprised the world by suggesting that the three very different kinds of marriage are all able to be satisfying and stable. He even says that "some conflict and disagreement are crucial for a marriage's long-term success" (*Why Marriages Succeed or Fail* [New York: Simon & Schuster, 1994], p. 173). The one factor that predicts that a marriage will last is not that the marriage is of a certain kind; it is that husband and wife share five times as many positives as negatives with each other. Some negatives are inevitable, even necessary! But the couples that are likely to last know how to fill their relationship with positives. That is the spirit of repentance. "In order to make our relationship better, I will work to find the good in my partner."

One of the best ways to make marriage more positive is by making conflicts and differences more oriented toward solutions and less toward blame. People who have been married several years often have characteristic patterns of conflict. Can you identify situations that usually set you off? What assumptions do you have that make the situation so toxic? Do you assume that your spouse should know better? Do you assume that he or she should be more aware of your needs? Can you change your assumptions? Can you see things from your spouse's perspective? Can you express your needs in a request? Can you find ways to make creative use of your differences?

The Lord has set a very high standard for our marital relationships. He counseled that the relationship be like that between Christ and the Church. Christ not only cares about the Church, he devotes himself to its progress. He "gave himself for it." (See Ephesians 5:22–25.) He acts as an advocate. What a beautiful pattern for our married relationships.

My sweetheart, Nancy, has an extraordinary ability to make creative use of difficult situations. On one occasion, the decision to help a new friend cash a check cost our family $500 when the friend disappeared and the check turned out to be bad. Nancy has never been one to blame others. We mused together that the money was our tuition for night school in business. No complaining. No blame. No pointless anger. Just quiet musings about the unexpected ways that we learn the lessons of life.

My life has been blessed profoundly by Nancy's willingness to find the good in every situation. She does not blame. She finds solutions. I continue to learn from her example. Usually my first reactions to disappointment are indignation, anger, and blame. But I am learning to think about solving problems rather than asking Nancy to meet all my needs. Maybe I will have mastered the skill by our fiftieth wedding anniversary. Maybe in the next life.

For the principle of repentance to work, we must be willing to take the perspective of our partner or "walk in their moccasins," as we say. The wisest partners ask good questions and are willing to listen. "How do you feel about that?" "What do you think is the solution?" A willingness to understand forms a strong foundation for loving relationships. Repentance means that we take personal responsibility to make our relationships better.

Charity is the third principle that has particular application to marriage. The world tends to think of benevolent giving as charity. In the Church we say that charity is the pure love of Christ. But charity is very different from love as we usually think of it.

Our culture generally defines love as "a profoundly tender, passionate affection for another person, esp. when based on sexual attraction" (*Random House Webster's College Dictionary* [New York: Random House, 1995], pp. 804–805). That definition is full of feeling. It is somewhat like the media image of love, which is blatantly sexual. Two people who are filled with desire and passion are clearly in love, if you believe the media image.

But God instructs us to love one another as he has loved us. His kind of love is called charity. It is the pure love of Christ: from Christ, for Christ, like Christ. Should we be surprised when his curriculum for every one of us requires that we love as he loves? His love is very unusual. It does not ask, "Would you be willing to meet my needs, and then I will do something nice for you?" It does not ask, "Shall we be nice to each other?" Rather it asks, "How can I bless you?" Charity is essential to successful marriage relationships.

To have the great spiritual gift of charity requires a spiritual process, the same process involved in all spiritual growth. We acknowledge our weakness and imperfection. We use faith, repentance, and covenants. We struggle to do what we know how to do. And we ask for a divine outpouring. We both forgive and ask for forgiveness. At those times when we do not feel charitable, we ask ourselves, "What would I do if I felt charity?" We can act the part. The feelings will follow.

I think of the time when Nancy asked me to help her with the ward Relief Society newsletter. She asked just as I was dashing off on a two-day business trip. I responded by observing that the newsletter had already waited several weeks. Why was I supposed to break into my pressing meetings because of her procrastination? My attitude was clearly not charitable. It was hostile. I might have said: "I am feeling a lot of pressure right now. Is there a chance that I could look at the newsletter with you on Friday?" This response is solution-oriented rather than blame-oriented. It is kinder and more charitable. Much of the difference between a hostile and a charitable response is not in the words. The difference is in the attitude. Charity is the attitude of blessing.

Of course, marriage is not merely a string of battles. There are times when we feel profoundly appreciative of and close with our partners. Unfortunately, we usually do not make those feelings prominent. We are wise to cherish, celebrate, and communicate the times of greatest affection. In a telestial world that provides so many challenges, the times of greatest affection may be the best indicators of the true quality of the relationship.

There is a surprise in the process for developing the gift of charity. We may suppose that we can will ourselves to be charitable. But the Lord recommends a very different process: "Charity is the pure love of Christ, and it endureth forever; and whoso is found possessed of it at the last day, it shall be well with him. Wherefore, my beloved brethren, pray unto the Father with all the energy of heart, that ye may be filled with this love, which he hath bestowed upon all who are true followers of his Son, Jesus

Christ; that ye may become the sons of God; that when he shall appear we shall be like him, for we shall see him as he is; that we may have this hope; that we may be purified even as he is pure." (Moroni 7:47–48.)

We are filled with the pure love of Christ as we try to be his followers and as we pray with all the energy of our souls. We have the pure love of Christ only as we are filled with him. So, if we are seeking a divine partnership, we should expect to have to bridle our passions. Anger and annoyance do not lead us to God. We also should expect to be talent scouts, looking for the fine, earnest, and noble in our partners. And we should expect to take Heavenly Father as a partner. "Nevertheless neither is the man without the woman, neither the woman without the man, in the Lord" (1 Corinthians 11:11). Such is the path to marital joy.

Eight

FIDELITY

Let thy soul delight in thy spouse.
—*See D&C 25:14*

Marriage is ordained of God (see D&C 49:15). It can be the most blessed and holy state known to mortals. It can be a hint of a glorious home on high. It can be joyous.

But "it must needs be, that there is an opposition in all things" (2 Nephi 2:11). It is common for us to marry someone who is perfectly suited to both bless us and to aggravate us. When a man was asked by his marriage counselor what first attracted him to his wife, he replied, "Her forthrightness and frankness." When asked why he now wanted to leave her, he replied, "Her forthrightness and frankness."

Often we are not wise enough to realize that the very behaviors that annoy us in our spouses may be vital to balancing our strengths and to helping us grow. A spouse's qualities become faults when they do not meet our needs. Then the faults become the focus of the relationship. And a person may wonder if it was a mistake to marry this stubborn, selfish person. Conflict and disappointment can become the theme of the relationship.

Father seems to have intended that we be aggravated. He wants us to learn to understand others, to accept them with their faults, to value them for their qualities, and to be aware of our own frailties. He wants us to love more than to correct. He wants us to learn how to see beyond our own needs to the needs of our partners.

The first test of a marriage may come with frustrated expectations. "Any good wife should know to . . ." "I don't understand why my husband doesn't . . ." The situation is worsened when spouses fail to discuss their differences, try to understand their partners' points of view, and find common ground. It is normal to feel frustrations, even big frustrations, with our marriages at times. The healthy response is to find ways to have a better relationship as a result of what is learned from the frustrations.

This is a good point to talk about the devil. He loves unrest and discontent. He loves "to interrupt [our] rejoicings" (Alma 30:22). He wants us to feel unsettled. It is clear that the devil's miserable cause is advanced by a nagging feeling that our marital relationship is not good. It keeps us from committing ourselves, from giving wholeheartedly to our spouses. It keeps us from solving problems. It also opens the door for infidelity.

A good friend taught me a lot about the subtle process that Satan uses. She is an earnest, married Latter-day Saint. She caught me at a social gathering to tell me of a great friendship she had developed with a man in her ward. She and he enjoyed great discussions about the gospel. Sometimes he called her from work. Occasionally they met downtown for lunch. He bought her little gifts. She told me how much she enjoyed her companionship with the man. I was worried. Then she told me how good the man was with children and how she wished her husband would be as sensitive. Then I knew.

The devil had carefully woven her discontent about her husband together with her affection for another man. The effect was devastating to her marriage. She was trying to find some way to leave her husband while still doing all she believed was right. It is a damned-if-you-do and damned-if-you-don't situation. She does not enjoy her marriage and family. Yet she can't find any way to have what she thinks she wants. She is trapped. She is right where the devil wants her. She is miserable.

The devil's methods for tricking us are predictable. Trouble starts with behaviors that seem very innocent. We do good, helpful things: supporting a troubled neighbor, sharing gospel ideas with a ward member, working closely with another person on a ward activity, listening to the troubles of a coworker. All of these kindnesses are good. But the trouble begins as a person starts to feel responsible for or very close to someone who is not his or her marriage partner. An affection is growing that claims part of the heart that belongs only to the spouse.

President Spencer W. Kimball has said:

"Thou shalt love thy wife with *all* thy heart, and shall cleave unto her and none else." ([D&C] 42:22. Italics added.)

And, when the Lord says *all* thy heart, it allows for no sharing nor dividing nor depriving. . . . The words *none else* eliminate everyone and everything. The spouse then becomes preeminent in the life of the husband or wife. . . .

Marriage presupposes total allegiance and total fidelity. Each spouse takes the partner with the understanding that he or she gives self totally to the spouse: all the heart, strength, loyalty, honor, and affection with all dignity. Any divergence is sin—any sharing the heart is transgression. As we should have "an eye single to the glory of God" so should we have an eye, an ear, a heart single to the marriage and the spouse and family. ("Spouses and None Else," *Improvement Era,* December 1962, p. 928.)

The covenant we make with God to avoid all sexual relations outside of marriage precludes not only physical but also romantic relationships outside of marriage, even if they are only mental or emotional.

Elder Gene R. Cook has said that we do not have the right to stimulate or be stimulated by anyone who is not our spouse ("The Eternal Nature of the Law of Chastity," address, 1989, Ricks College, Rexburg, Idaho). In the early stages of extramarital flirting, the intoxicating feeling of someone's affection and the sense of our innocence may blind us to the seriousness of our situation.

The unfaithfulness moves to a more serious and dangerous stage of unfaithfulness when one or both of the people declare their relationship special. They would never dream of doing anything immoral or improper. But they increasingly make excuses to see each other. They plan their schedules to assure that they will be together. Cards, notes, and gifts are exchanged.

One telltale indicator that a relationship has moved to a dangerous stage is worrying about what people may say about the time or affection that you are sharing with the other person. Another indicator is making excuses or telling lies to hide the time or resources spent on the other person. Both are messages from your conscience that you are doing something wrong.

At this stage, sacred covenants have already been violated and permanent damage lurks. The rightful place of spouse in a person's heart is crowded by affections for another person. At this stage of unfaithfulness the person is especially likely to be finding fault with his or her spouse. The spouse is compared to the special friend: "I wish my husband were as good with children as Fred." "I wish my wife were as alert and interesting as Mandy."

At this stage a person is misled enough to start weaving fantasies: "Maybe the Lord will take my husband so that John and I can be together." "Somehow, someday the Lord will work out this beautiful relationship for us." Ouch! The Lord does not murder selected children in order to satisfy our whims and lustful fantasies. He asks instead that we learn to love and to overlook faults in our spouse. He asks that we honor commitments and strengthen our partners. He asks that we be as good and kind to our partners as we would have them be to us.

This stage of unfaithfulness can be a full-blown addiction even if physical intimacies have not been shared. The treatment for it can be wrenching. But rationalization that it is not a problem and that we can handle it may only delay the pain and increase the risk of further, permanent damage to the family.

The final stage of unfaithfulness begins officially with the showing of any physical affection. It is easy for special friends to justify a squeeze. Even a kiss seems innocent enough. The friends may be determined to avoid immorality at all costs. They may think that full sexual expression is not even to be considered. But intoxication with the pleasures of romance make the insistent and powerful pleading of biological urges more and more difficult to ignore. Even if a couple exercises enough restraint to avoid having sex, the damage to family relations that comes from divided loyalties and ugly dishonesty is terrific and tragic. Trust is destroyed. Covenants, with all of their glorious promises, are wasted. "And thus the devil cheateth their souls, and leadeth them away carefully down to hell" (2 Nephi 28:21).

But it does not have to be that way. At any point in the process, we can repent. The more time and emotion that we have invested in our fantasy, the harder it is to get out. We may try to kid ourselves into thinking that we can somehow honor our covenants and look forward to the promised day when we can have our soul mate. But covenants without our hearts committed to them are meaningless. The devil must roar with laughter as he observes us feeling confined by our sacred covenants while yearning for something that does not and cannot satisfy. Wickedness never was and never will be happiness (see Alma 41:10).

Latter-day Saints should be alert to the predictable temptations that Satan uses to break up marriages. We should monitor our behavior and our feelings closely. By being alert to the danger signs, we can prevent the problems that begin so innocently but end so disastrously. There are several guidelines that can help prevent trouble:

1. Never make excuses to spend time alone with a person of the opposite sex who is not your spouse.

2. Take responsibility for the messages that you give. You do not have the right to be cute or flirty with anyone but your spouse. Do not use cards, gifts, or charm to win the affection of anyone who is not your spouse.

3. Do not allow your heart to dwell on anyone. Push daydreaming of any person but your spouse out of your mind promptly. When you are worried about someone's well-being, pray for him or her and trust Heavenly Father to care for him or her. The untangling of excuses and emotional dependence can be the hardest part of overcoming the addiction.

4. If you find yourself making excuses for continuing the relationship, you are addicted. Get help. Talk with your bishop or stake president. Seek out the help of friends who will help you overcome your addiction.

5. Spend more enjoyable time with your spouse. Have weekly dates doing those things that you enjoy together. Find ways to improve your relationship. Be patient. Recognize that many of our frustrations with our spouses are built on the false assumption that they ought to be a certain way. Change your assumptions. Recognize that even the best marriages have more and less satisfying times. Be patient. Be true to your covenants. Enjoy your partner as he or she is. It is easy to believe that things will never be right with your spouse. Trust the Lord that he can heal all wounds.

6. Renew your spiritual efforts. Turn to the Lord in prayer. Ask for strength to put temptation out of your mind. Fill your empty places with service, scripture study, and love for your family.

7. Don't set yourself up for failure. Don't allow yourself to spend time alone with the person. Avoiding is better than resisting. Make your spouse a partner in all helping.

While the grass may seem very green on the other side of the fence, if we tend our own little patch, even with all its weeds and rocks, we will find a joy that passes understanding. If we sit on the fence and dream, we will lose even our allotted garden spot. And the devil knows that. We should be prepared for Satan's attacks. He offers love and fun and a satisfying life. But it is a lie. He wants to get us to violate our covenants. But he has no joy to deliver despite his grandiose promises. He is the master of misery. That is all he has to offer.

If we have been unwise enough to have been caught in a trap, we may repent. When we honor covenants made with our Heavenly Father, we are always blessed. Always. Sometimes Father's process requires us to be patient. Sometimes he requires us to bear discomfort. But he always blesses those who obey eternal laws. And the blessings are in incredible disproportion to the price we have paid. "Be glad in the Lord, and rejoice, ye righteous: and shout for joy, all ye that are upright in heart" (Psalm 32:11).

Nine

LEARNING HOW TO PARENT
FROM THE PERFECT PARENT

Be ye therefore perfect,
even as your Father which is in heaven is perfect.
—Matthew 5:48

Charlie's troubled question made me think. "If Heavenly Father thinks raising children is so important, why hasn't he given us any instructions in scriptures on how to do it?" It is natural that Charlie should ask such a question. He has a large family with lots of struggles. Also, he is a man who loves the scriptures and is earnestly seeking answers from them.

After I reflected for a moment, the answer to his question seemed clear to me: All of scripture tells us about a perfect Father's dealing with his children. Every story, every episode in scripture teaches us how to parent if we learn from his perfect example.

Already one lesson about Heavenly Father's style is apparent. He is subtle. He does not stand in our faces and bark commands. He graciously offers a library of ideas. He invites us to explore, to learn, and to make our own unique application of his example.

I think of the way the Lord taught Elijah (see 1 Kings 18–19). After the wonderful and public manifestation of the Lord's power on Mount Carmel in which a doused sacrifice was consumed by divine fire, Elijah expected the people to be different, wiser, more committed. When Queen Jezebel reacted to the experience by threatening his life, Elijah was devastated. I imagine him thinking: "The people don't get it. Nothing works. I give up." He went into the desert and asked the Lord to take his life.

The Lord might have angrily chided Elijah for his lack of vision. Or he might have called someone else in his place. But the Lord did something very different.

The Lord asked Elijah to meet him in Horeb, the mount of God, the same sacred place where Moses was taught by a tutoring Father. The trip to Horeb was a forty-day journey. So Elijah started off on the trying trek. He was sustained by food from an angel. (Another lesson about the Lord: When he asks us to make a journey to meet him where he will bless us and teach us, he sustains us every step of the way!)

The Lord asked Elijah his purpose in coming to Horeb. Elijah poured out his tale of woe again in words similar to these: "After the marvelous show of power, the people still don't get it. I've had it. Let me die." A lesser being might have lost patience. But the Lord said, in essence, "Elijah, come and stand with me. Let's talk." And the Lord caused a strong wind to tear up the mountain. Such a strong wind must have left Elijah feeling helpless and frightened. And then the Lord let the unspoken question hang in the air: "Elijah, am I that amazing wind?" The answer was clear. He was not. Then the Lord sent a terrifying earthquake. Again, the same question, and the same answer. Then consuming fire, devouring all in its path—like that sent at Mount Carmel to show the Lord's power. The same question. The same answer. Even consuming fire is not the Lord's essence.

After the three amazing shows of power, the scriptural account reports, "And after the fire a still small voice." The still small voice! Elijah learned that the Lord is not essentially a violent manifestation. He is not essentially frightening power. He is the quiet message in our souls. This is where we are to find the Lord's message: on the fleshy tablets of our hearts.

Again the Lord asked Elijah why he had come. Again Elijah gave his plaintive reply, though it must now have seemed hollow. Again, the Lord did not remonstrate. Having humbled and taught his prophet, he now redirected him in words like these: "Elijah, I have precious children still among Israel who have not worshiped Baal. They need a leader. A leader who knows. Please go back and teach and bless them. And prepare Elisha so that, when the time comes for you to return home, he will be able to carry on the work."

Wow. What an example of perfect parenting!

In the struggles of life, the people of Israel did not get it. Elijah did not get it. Do we? Do we look for dramatic answers when the answers are in our hearts? Do we hear the Lord's gentle, teaching messages in our lives? Do we respond to his invitations to serve and to have joy?

In all of the process with Elijah, the Lord did not cajole, complain, coax, or wheedle. He invited and he taught. I think there is a great lesson there, subtle but powerful. A perfect example of perfect parenting. Father might well encourage those of us who are struggling as parents to go and do likewise.

Some people point to an Old Testament God who is cruel, demanding, jealous, and punitive. I suspect that we discover the God we are prepared to know. As I study the scriptures, I find a God who gives every opportunity, every invitation, every enticement and who acts strongly only when his children stubbornly refuse to change *and* are robbing others of their right to choose. Even to hardened sinners the Lord's "hand is stretched out still" (2 Nephi 15:25). He is relentless in his redemptiveness.

He offers us inexpressible joy. Such joy is to be found in the love of God, which is "most desirable above all things . . . and the most joyous" (1 Nephi 11:22–23). "Behold, he sendeth an invitation unto all men, for the arms of mercy are extended towards them, and he saith: Repent, and I will receive you" (Alma 5:33).

Even for the wicked, the message essentially is: "When you keep yourself outside my love, you will be miserable. In a troubled world, the only safe haven is in my arms. Please come. Come home to my love so I can bless you." That gentle message is angering to the child who insists: "I don't want to do it your way. I want to do it my way."

Even then the Lord does not spank us or send us to our rooms. Nor does he turn his back on us. As in the parable of the prodigal, he waits at the gate. Waits. Waits. Waits. And when he sees us turning back toward home, he runs to us, wraps us in his divine love, places the royal ring on our finger, and makes a celebration feast. Even though we have been so foolish and wasteful. So wayward. So prodigal. (See Luke 15:11–32.)

That is exactly how I have experienced the Father. Even when I was suffering the consequences of terrible mistakes and I impertinently cried out, "Why? Why must I suffer so?" he did not cajole or lecture. He taught me. He comforted me. And he busied me in service. The Father loves his children, even when we are weak, narrow, and selfish.

As mortal parents, we will not be as infinitely patient as he. But we can still learn how to handle difficult challenges from his example. "Surely," his example says, "teaching children is better than hurting them."

Enoch also learned about God's remarkable love for his children (see Moses 7). The Lord spoke face-to-face with faithful Enoch and showed him the human saga. Enoch was engrossed. When he turned to the Lord he was astonished to discover that he was weeping. Enoch remonstrated, essentially saying: "You are God. You have all power. You made everything. How can you cry? Why do you cry?" The Lord's kind answer was along these lines: "Enoch, these are my children we are seeing. I love them. Shouldn't the heavens weep seeing that my children should suffer?" Enoch himself was then engulfed in the tragic realization of misery. He wept. And he refused to be comforted through the continuing drama until the Lord showed him the ultimate triumph of the Savior's redemption. "And Enoch . . . walked with God" (Moses 7:69).

The Lord asks: "Have I any pleasure at all that the wicked should die? . . . and not that he should return from his ways, and live?" (Ezekiel 18:23.)

The Lord is no hardened warden. He weeps with us when we suffer because of our bad decisions. "For we have not an high priest which cannot be touched with the feeling of our infirmities; but was in all points tempted like as we are, yet without sin. Let us therefore come boldly unto the throne of grace, that we may obtain mercy, and find grace to help in time of need." (Hebrews 4:15–16.)

Having borne the pain of sins that he did not commit, the Lord understands the pain, heartache, and disappointment of sin. He weeps when we suffer, because he understands. And he is anxious to move us on to growth, joy, and service.

That is the God I have experienced, a Father who so seriously respects our right to govern our own lives that he is willing to allow us to struggle, to hurt ourselves and each other, to shake our fists at him. He stands and waits at the gate. Patiently. Lovingly. Longingly. Inviting us to come home. Inviting us to be healed, taught, and blessed.

He does not have to rush in to stop every misdeed. He keeps sending the message of love. He allows us to make decisions. He faithfully stands by, knowing that when we have learned the lessons of life we will be ready to be redeemed. Ultimately we will discover how we need him. Oh, how we need him!

So what might we learn from the Father's perfect example of parenting?

First, he loves us. He loves us deeply, totally, compassionately, patiently, unconditionally. He is involved and committed.

It is not natural for us to love as he loves. But if we let his Spirit fill us, we may truly love one another as he loves. At those times when we do not feel loving, we might do well to ask, How would he see my struggling child? How would he treat this troubled one?

Second, he allows us to make decisions. He respects our right to govern our own lives. But he is not impartial. He sets us up for success. He does not give us challenges that are too great for us. He provides guidance. He teaches. He provides the Holy Ghost to point the way. And when we have made mistakes, he heals us. For each of us he has customized a lifetime of appropriate growth opportunities.

We are wise to study the scriptures in order to learn from him. Are there scripture stories that regularly fill you with joy? What can you learn about the Father's parenting from them?

In your own life, have you felt his patience, gentleness, and goodness? Have you felt, as did Lehi, "encircled about eternally in the arms of his love" (2 Nephi 1:15)? Reflect on your best experiences with the Father. Feast on his love. Think how you can provide gentle loving for your family members.

Third, he teaches. Part of the teaching comes from the natural consequences woven into the laws of life. We discover that there is no joy in sin. Nor is there any misery in our relationship with God. When we are humble enough to learn, he comes to us. He shows us beautiful truths, the truths that are suited to our needs. He does it all subtly. Kindly. Wisely.

Can we learn to work with our children as the Lord did with Elijah and help them learn the sweet lessons of life?

Fourth, he invites us to join him in service. Just as he sent Elijah back to Israel to teach and bless, so he sends us out to love and serve. It is remarkable that he allows us with all our imperfections to represent him as missionaries, teachers, and parents!

We might invite our children to join us in visiting the widows, cooking for the hungry, and providing shelter for the homeless and love for the weary. How can we as families learn to have more joy in service?

Oh, that we could be as good as he! He invites us: "Learn of me, and listen to my words; walk in the meekness of my Spirit, and you shall have peace in me" (D&C 19:23).

It might be nice if he would provide a step-by-step manual for parenting. He does not. Rather, he invites us to study his doings, learn from his words, feel his Spirit, and follow his perfect example. Truly, Heavenly Father knows how to bless his children. "Thou wilt shew me the path of life: in thy presence is fulness of joy; at thy right hand there are pleasures for evermore" (Psalm 16:11).

Ten

THINKING BIG

Out of the abundance of the heart the mouth speaketh.
—Matthew 12:34

The largeness or smallness of our souls has a big impact on our ability to experience joy and to share love.

An older widow was in the habit of going to the grocery store every day. She bought just a few items, hardly more than a day's supply. The clerks thought this odd because most people buy groceries for several days at a time. One day one of the clerks was bold enough to inquire, "Why do you buy only a few things each day?"

"Well," she replied, "it's just that I'm a widow and I live with my nephew and I can't stand him. When I die I don't want to leave him any groceries."

So human. In each of us is a part that says, "I'll be darned if I'm going to give anything to someone I don't like. He or she doesn't deserve it!" That is smallness of soul.

I love the story of an unusual Little League coach. He had a team that just couldn't get the idea of baseball. He spent much of their practices just teaching the boys about which way to run around the bases. They lost game after game. There was one little boy in particular who never caught the ball or hit it in any practice or in any game. The team arrived at a dramatic moment in the final game of the season: last inning, two outs, down by one run. The little boy who had never hit the ball or caught it came up to bat. The team figured the game was over, and they started bagging up the bats and balls. But somehow, miraculously, this little kid connected and got on first base. The team was ecstatic because next up to bat was the team slugger. If the team slugger drove in the little fellow on base and himself, they would win their only win of the season. What a great way to end an otherwise disappointing season! The team slugger did what he did so well: he made a solid hit toward right field. The little kid on first base who had never hit the ball and never caught it was a little confused about the rules of baseball. But he figured that the right thing to do was to head toward second base. So he took off. But halfway there he saw the ball coming toward him. This confused him. So he caught it, thereby making the final out against his own team. Imagine the perplexed coach and team. After reflecting for a moment, the coach turned to the team and said: "Cheer. This kid has never before hit the ball or caught it. He just did both in the same inning."

Bigness. Generosity. Kindness. Graciousness. Hopefully, we have all experienced it. Bigness feels good. It leads us to joy.

"How delightful is the company of generous people, who overlook trifles and keep their minds instinctively fixed on whatever is good and positive in the world about them. People of small caliber are always carping. They are bent on showing their own superiority, their knowledge or prowess or good breeding. But magnanimous people have no vanity, they have no jealousy, and they feed on the true and the solid wherever they find it. And, what is more, they find it everywhere." (Van Wyck Brooks in *A Chilmark Miscellany* [New York: Dutton, n.d.].)

Jesus provides us a marvelous contrast of bigness and smallness with his experience in the home of Simon the Pharisee (see Luke 7:36–50). Simon invited Jesus to dine with him apparently out of some sense of curiosity. He showed no courtesy or deference for his divine guest. As they were dining in the courtyard open to the street, a sinful woman with an alabaster box of ointment approached Jesus tenderly. The woman "stood at his feet behind him weeping, and began to wash his feet with tears, and did wipe them with the hairs of her head, and kissed his feet, and anointed them with the ointment" (Luke 7:38).

Sneering Simon was repulsed with the woman's presence and disgusted that Jesus did not recognize her low character and send her away. The kind, gentle Master drew their attention to the irony of the situation by telling the story of two debtors, one who owed five hundred pence and the other who owed fifty pence. Both were forgiven their debts. Jesus asked, Which of them was more grateful? Presumably it was the person forgiven the greater debt, Simon conceded. And then Jesus confronted Simon with his smallness: "Seest thou this woman? I entered into thine house, thou gavest me no water for my feet: but she hath washed my feet with tears, and wiped them with the hairs of her head. Thou gavest me no kiss: but this woman since the time I came in hath not ceased to kiss my feet. My head with oil thou didst not anoint: but this woman hath anointed my feet with ointment. Wherefore I say unto thee, Her sins, which are many, are forgiven; for she loved much. . . . And he said unto her, Thy sins are forgiven." (Luke 7:44–48.)

What a dramatic contrast! Simon sat smugly judging the woman. The sinful woman was forgiven because of her whole-souled love for the Redeemer. But even after experiencing the example of the Master's bigness, the small, grudging, judgmental Pharisees could react only by asking in their hearts, "Who does he think he is, presuming to forgive sins?"

Maybe the Pharisees were big in the community. Powerful. Prominent. Seemingly righteous. But their hearts were shriveled, small, cruel, and empty.

The sinful woman was small, shunned, insignificant in the community. But her heart was full of devotion, love, gratitude, and hope. Jesus keeps surprising us by reminding us that he does not measure as the world measures. He measures the bigness of our hearts.

For each of us, the matter of bigness and smallness is put into personal perspective by the story of the unforgiving debtor (see Matthew 18:23–35). A servant, called before his master to account for a debt that would equal millions of dollars today begged for mercy and was forgiven the debt. But when the servant met a man who owed him the equivalent of a few dollars, who likewise petitioned for mercy, he had him thrown into prison. The message is gentle but clear. Each of us goes to the King to be forgiven vast debts. He gladly forgives us. How ungracious it is when we are small, stingy, and unwilling to forgive our fellow travelers their puny debts to us.

The Lord asks: "Shouldest not thou also have had compassion on thy fellowservant, even as I had pity on thee?" (Matthew 18:33.)

We have good examples of such bigness. For example, Nephi, after much tribulation with his brothers, said: "And it came to pass that I did frankly forgive them all that they had done" (1 Nephi 7:21).

It's probably easy to be big when we are feeling good about life, good about ourselves, and good about things in general. It's easier to be big when we're feeling good. But when we're tired and discouraged and frustrated, when we're without love and hope, it's hard to be big.

Rousseau used to write glowing essays about the inherent goodness of children. But his children still annoyed him. He sent his five children to the orphanage. (See A. Synnott, "Little Angels, Little Devils: A Sociology of Children," *Canadian Review of Sociology and Anthropology,* 20(1):79–95.)

There are several things we can do to encourage bigness in ourselves. The most important may be to keep ourselves filled with a sense of Heavenly Father's goodness. The reading of scriptures should not be done to satisfy some demanding ogre in heaven. It is a way of getting to know the Father. We can see him working in scriptures. We can get acquainted with him as we read of his efforts to redeem his children. We can also see him acting in our own lives.

We are more likely to be big when we see as the Father sees, notice and remember the good, understand people's noblest intentions. I think it was just such an understanding that I felt one evening with little Andy. Nancy was away at a meeting, and I was watching the children. While I was washing the dishes, I did not notice the great danger sign familiar to all mothers: the kids were quiet. When I finished the dishes, I entered the family room to find that Andy had discovered the finger paints on the bottom shelf of the bookcase. The bold swatches of brilliant red, yellow, green, and blue were breathtaking on our new carpet. On that occasion I was calm enough to consider: "What does this mean to Andy? Is he trying to torment me? No. Is he merely exploring and enjoying his toddler world? I think so." So I explained to him the advantage of finger painting on slick paper that can be hung on the fridge. "Ohhhhh!" said Andy in a delighted way. And we cleaned up the carpet together.

I do better at bigness when I remember that Father has invited us to help and love each other. Sometimes we unwittingly promote smallness in our families. For example, because we want our children to learn responsibility, we are usually quite firm in our schedule of doing the dishes. We soon found that our children were very quick to demand that the scheduled person do the dishes even on evenings that were overwhelmingly busy for the assigned child. While we do want to teach our children responsibility, we don't want to teach them smallness. So Nancy and I have tried to apply lessons of bigness to getting the dishes done. While we normally expect our children to do their dishes on their appointed day, when they are unusually stressed, we volunteer: "May I do the dishes for you tonight? Can we help you any other way? Is there anyone in the family who would like to help?" Responsibility is important. So are compassion and cooperation.

While it is normal to occasionally feel angry, peevish, and out-of-sorts, we can learn to handle our feelings in nondestructive ways. For example, I have found that any correcting I do when I am angry is likely to be destructive and unhelpful. So I try not to correct when I am angry. Some evenings I am so cross that I isolate myself to my bedroom to work. When I am feeling tired, troubled, angry, cross, or irritated, I avoid making important or sensitive decisions. When I am feeling hopeful, loving, and generous is a much better time to make decisions.

We have found that humor is one way of delivering our messages in unhurtful ways. One of our family uses of humor is known as "training sessions." For example, if I have found that we are unexpectedly out of toilet paper, I am inclined to be angry, to gather the family, and to lecture about thrift. Instead I call the whole family to the bathroom. We gather in a small circle as I tell them that, due to excessive waste of valuable paper, we have developed a new policy. In the future all paper will be kept in a locked booth outside the bathroom. In order to get any, they must complete a form in triplicate justifying each square they request. Forms must be completed twenty-four hours in advance. Then their request will be considered by their mother and me. If we deem it justified, one of us will issue the paper.

Of course the kids laugh at me. But they get the message. And I have not insulted or hurt them. Sometimes we must find creative ways to get past our normal, telestial smallness.

Sometimes in a family there is one child who is in trouble a lot. Probably that child is not well understood. Maybe a strong will puts him or her at odds with the other family members. That is the child who most needs our love, understanding, and prayers.

Think of the remarkable example of the Savior. He regularly surprised all observers by reaching out to the least deserving. The Samaritan woman at the well. The adulterers. The lepers. The publicans. Never in the history of this earth has there been such a great example of bigness!

When we are gracious and kind while still having high expectations, we are likely to develop big-hearted children. That is the trick—taking care of small things without forgetting the eternal things. As Paul said, "The letter killeth, but the spirit giveth life" (2 Corinthians 3:6).

It feels good to be big.

Eleven

HUMAN NATURE:
WHAT MAKES PEOPLE CHANGE?

Every spirit of man was innocent in the beginning.
—D&C 93:38

We all have assumptions about how to make people change. Percy Burrup, a professor of education at Brigham Young University, used to say, "You can't make people do something, but you can make them sorry they didn't." Much of our judicial system—and our parenting behavior—is based on the simple premise, "If you don't do what I say, I can make you suffer."

But consider your own experience. Is the avoidance of punishment the primary factor in deciding your behavior? It may have a significant role, but it is probably not the whole story. We try to avoid punishment. But we also seek peace, companionship, purpose, and love.

Consider three different views of what causes people to change. Each of these views has natural assumptions and parenting implications.

The first view is that people are basically bad. Sigmund Freud said: "I have found little that is good about human beings. In my experience most of them are trash." (Quoted in Robert Byrne, sel., *1,911 Best Things Anybody Ever Said* [1988], p. 194.) Trash. Selfish and self-serving. Freud was not alone in that view. John Calvin, the religious reformer, believed that people are born in sin and prone to evil, and that strict restraint and strong punishment are necessary to control human nature. And he practiced what he preached. There was a case brought to his attention in which a young boy had struck his parents. Calvin had the boy beheaded. (See P. Hobsbaum, "Calvinism in Action: The Superego Triumphant," *Hudson Review* 25 [1972]: 23–50.) Apparently submission was valued above life. Calvin's view of life and service has been characterized in the following way: "Serving God is no child's play. It is no joy, no pleasure. It is a grim, stark, gloomy business." (Henry Thomas and Dana Lee Thomas, *Living Biographies of Religious Leaders* [Garden City, New York: Garden City Publishing, 1942], p. 190.)

Another Christian reformer, John Wesley, had a remarkable life. His mother, Susannah Wesley, believed that it was important to subdue the willfulness of a child. Fortunately she wrote much about her parenting philosophy, such as: "Whenever a child is corrected, it must be conquered; and this will be no hard matter to do if it be not grown headstrong by too much indulgence. And when the will of a child is totally subdued, and it is brought to revere and stand in awe of the parents, then a great many childish follies and inadvertencies may be passed by." (In Nehemiah Curnock, ed., vol. 3, *The Journal of the Rev. John Wesley, A. M.* [London: Robert Culley, 1909].)

The child must submit to the parents as part of and preparation for submitting to God, according to this view. But this bitter tree bears bitter fruit. John Wesley wrestled most of his life with the feeling that he was not quite acceptable to God. That was painful for a minister of the gospel. Eventually he got to the point where he believed he was justified in the eyes of God. But even then he felt no joy. "Justification without Joy" is the fitting title for his psychohistory (see R. L. Moore, "Justification without Joy: Psychohistorical Reflections on John Wesley's Childhood and Conversion," *History of Childhood Quarterly* 2(1):31–52). Consider the cruel irony: Redeemed of God, but miserable.

If our parenting is oriented toward subjection and submission, we are likely to have children who have little sense of self and who are less able to experience joy. They have not felt respected, valued, and loved. It will be harder for them to love.

If a parent believes that human nature is basically bad, then that parent must make lots of rules and promptly punish for infractions of the rules. The abundant weeds of human nature must not be allowed to flourish.

Even some parents who do not believe that children are basically bad treat children as if they believed it. And the message gets through to the children: "You cannot be trusted."

People who believe that children are basically bad may worry a lot about spoiling a child. Human nature must be tortured, reformed, controlled. One father with such a view (see Claude Steiner, *Scripts People Live: Transactional Analysis of Life Scripts* [New York: Grove Press, Inc., 1974], pp. 58–59) determined to deny his daughter anything she wanted and provide some other gift of equal value in order to avoid spoiling her. If she wanted a teddy bear, he would give her a doll. He consistently avoided giving her what she wanted. The girl learned that none of her wishes would be granted. She also learned that it was best never to let anyone know what she really wanted. Think how many problems that can make for her in marriage! Such strange distortions result when we start with ugly assumptions about human nature.

The view that people are basically bad is troublesome. Much of the Christian world has traditionally believed that we humans are all fundamentally depraved. But Latter-day Saint theology teaches that we are born innocent. We are enemies to God only if we let the flesh rule, only if we are unchanged by his Spirit. But his Spirit invites and entices us to be spiritual, to be changed, to be holy. Our true eternal nature is good.

"For the natural man is an enemy to God, and has been from the fall of Adam, and will be, forever and ever, unless he yields to the enticings of the Holy Spirit, and putteth off the natural man and becometh a saint through the atonement of Christ the Lord, and becometh as a child, submissive, meek, humble, patient, full of love, willing to submit to all things which the Lord seeth fit to inflict upon him, even as a child doth submit to his father" (Mosiah 3:19).

The revolutionary Latter-day Saint view about the fundamental innocence of children is very much in tune with modern scientific thinking. It is clear that there is part of us that is self-preserving and self-serving. (When there are four pieces of pie and five family members, I tend to think that I can resolve the problem by eating all four pieces.) Latter-day Saints call this bad side the natural man. But that may not be the most important or the most interesting part of our human natures. And the job of parenting is probably not to intimidate and torture that natural man but to turn away from the evil nature, giving heed to the spiritual.

The second view of human nature, the behavioristic view, is that people are basically clay or a blank slate. You can make them what you want. This view was very popular in American psychology for some decades. A leading proponent of the view was John B. Watson, who said: "Give me a dozen healthy infants, well-formed, and my own specified world to bring them up in and I'll guarantee to take any one at random and train him to become any type of specialist I might select—into a doctor, lawyer, artist, merchant-chief, and yes, even into beggar-man and thief, regardless of his talents, penchants, tendencies, abilities, vocations and race of ancestors" (quoted in D. Beekman, *The Mechanical Baby* [Westport, Connecticut: Lawrence Hill and Co., 1977], pp. 145–46).

Think about your own experience with children. Are you able to make a given child into anything you want? Are their personalities only a function of what they have been rewarded for?

In contrast to Watson's view, I think of my son Andy. When Andy was small, we read Bible stories together every morning before breakfast. We told the stories in our own words and supported them with illustrations. We read for several weeks about Moses and his leadership of the children of Israel. One particular morning we read about Moses leaving his people, never to be with them again in mortality. Then we had breakfast. In the middle of breakfast I turned to find that Andy was weeping. I was surprised. I asked, "Andy, what's wrong?" He said, "Dad"— and I thought his little heart would break with sobbing—"I'm going to miss Moses!"

Andy is a very tender boy. I couldn't ever train him to be cruel and heartless. He might be thoughtless or mischievous at times. But he never will and never could make a fine terrorist, thief, or destroyer.

John Watson is also famous for statements he made about how we should treat our children: "There is a sensible way of treating children. Treat them as though they were young adults. . . . Never hug and kiss them, never let them sit in your lap. If you must, kiss them once on the forehead when they say good night. Shake hands with them in the morning. Give them a pat on the head if they have made an extraordinarily good job of a difficult task . . . won't you then remember . . . that mother love is a dangerous instrument? An instrument which may inflict a never healing wound, a wound which may make infancy unhappy, adolescence a nightmare, an instrument which may wreck your adult son or daughter's vocational future and their chances for marital happiness." (*Psychological Care of Infant and Child* [New York: W. W. Norton and Co., 1928], pp. 81, 82, 87.)

Perhaps such cool detachment sounds sensible. But years of research have shown Watson to be completely mistaken. Detached objectivity is less useful for effective parenting than warm nurturing is. Watson's advice is not only at odds with decades of research but also with the gospel of Jesus Christ. I love the image conjured by a wise Lehi, who was about to die: "But behold, the Lord hath redeemed my soul from hell; I have beheld his glory, and I am encircled about eternally in the arms of his love" (2 Nephi 1:15). Encircled in the arms of love! What a great image for the ideal parent-child relationship! "Can a woman forget her sucking child, that she should not have compassion on the son of her womb? yea, they may forget, yet will I not forget thee. Behold, I have graven thee upon the palms of my hands; thy walls are continually before me." (Isaiah 49:15–16.) Such scriptural images of a loving parent are more in tune with the loving, nurturing spirit that researchers recommend today.

Of course we don't want to be unfair to the children-as-clay view. There is a part of every person that is malleable or moldable. If I get a speeding ticket every time I drive to work, I am likely to slow down or take the bus. But this view is clearly not the whole story. There is some part, the most important part, of our natures that is eternal. It is not shaped by incentives and punishments.

A third view is that people are basically good. Abraham Maslow and Carl Rogers are famous proponents of this view. Consider what Maslow said (see A. H. Maslow, *Motivation and Personality* [New York: Harper and Row, 1954]). If you provide food and shelter; safety; warm, caring relationships; and a feeling of value, something marvelous will come out of a person. He called it self-actualization. His view is very optimistic. It assumes that sickness is the result of basic development being thwarted. People who have good, supportive life experiences become self-directed and healthy people. Wellness is the natural outcome of normal development.

The recommendations for parents that come out of this view are very positive. Provide a safe, caring environment for your children. Let them explore. Help them discover the messages and missions inside themselves. They will become something wonderful!

The following observation by W. Somerset Maugham fits with this view: "The common idea that success spoils people by making them vain, egoistic and self-complacent is erroneous; on the contrary it makes them, for the most part, humble, tolerant and kind. Failure makes people bitter and cruel. Success improves the character of the man." (*The Maugham Reader* [Garden City, New York: Doubleday and Co., 1950], p. 598.) Apparently there is good inside the child that grows and develops as it experiences a nurturing environment. A sunflower seed will become a robust sunflower if provided with appropriate soil, water, and sunshine.

Note how different this is from the behavioristic or children-as-clay view. The extreme behaviorist would say, "Let's train this child to become something good by reinforcing good behavior and by ignoring or punishing bad behavior. The child will become nothing more nor less than I want and am able to make the child." Careful planning and manipulation by parents and other socializers is vitally important. In contrast, the view of human nature as basically good suggests that it is the parents' job to help children discover their gifts and to facilitate their development. That is a very big difference.

Of course it is important that we not reinforce bad behavior and make appreciation for good behavior unavailable. We can damage a child's best nature by insensitivity and carelessness.

Sandra Scarr, a respected child development researcher, has concluded that parents should provide plentiful opportunities for children and a supportive environment so that children can "become themselves" (S. Scarr, "Developmental Theories for the 1990s: Development and Individual Differences," *Child Development* 63:15). Become themselves—not what *we* make them. For people who believe in an eternal identity, that should be a familiar and comfortable concept. "What is man, that thou art mindful of him? and the son of man, that thou visitest him? For thou hast made him a little lower than the angels, and hast crowned him with glory and honour." (Psalm 8:4–5.)

Humans are basically good and godlike even if we do have some bad and some clay parts to our nature. There's part of us that is self-preserving, that would do whatever it takes to get what we want. Maybe that is the natural man. We also are partly clay, molded by experience. But there is also the good and noble part. Maybe that is our eternal spirit and that part of us where we have allowed God's Spirit to take up occupancy in us.

Father Lehi would also suggest that some children are harder to raise than others. But even for the hardest, our task as parents is to point them continually to the angels in their lives. When our children seem impossible, we might try to see them as Heavenly Father sees them: as extraordinary spirits confused by their distance from their eternal home and darkened by mistakes. We might also try to understand that the most sensitive spirits may sometimes be hurt the most readily and may require the most tender care.

Notice the remarkable insights about parenting that come from the Lord's counsel: "Every spirit of man was innocent in the beginning; and God having redeemed man from the fall, men became again, in their infant state, innocent before God. And that wicked one cometh and taketh away light and truth, through disobedience, from the children of men, and because of the tradition of their fathers. But I have commanded you to bring up your children in light and truth." (D&C 93:38–40.)

We start out innocent. Satan removes truth through getting us to disobey both Heavenly Father and our own eternal natures. We can teach our children to recognize and follow light and truth. That is the way. "After those days, saith the Lord, I will put my law in their inward parts, and write it in their hearts" (Jeremiah 31:33).

Each child has a spirit that is filled with a specific mission and visions of eternal possibilities. Our job as parents is not to impose our preferences on our children but to help them discover their unique missions and express those missions fully in their lives.

Our children need us to teach them how to recognize evil, avoid it, and go toward the light.

We must also teach them to turn away from the fears, resentments, and doubts that are a part of the natural man. And we can teach them to choose the right regardless of reward or punishment.

The view that people are basically good supports the recommendation that we should turn children to their inner, spiritual voices for answers. We should reason with them. We should listen to them. We should love them. We should look for the best in them.

We are not trying to tame or manipulate children. We are nurturing them so that they may fill the measure of their creation. That sounds right to me. It agrees with research findings. And most important, it agrees with the example and teachings of our Beloved Father.

Twelve

LOVE ONE ANOTHER: SKILLS IN EFFECTIVE PARENTING

The nearer we get to our heavenly Father, the more we are
disposed to look with compassion on perishing souls;
we feel that we want to take them upon our shoulders,
and cast their sins behind our backs.
—*Joseph Smith*

Love is a nice idea. Warmth, caring, closeness, sharing. The American definition of love seems to be, "Love is a feeling you feel you're gonna feel when you feel a feeling that you never felt before." The American ideal of love is full of golden light and warm feelings.

But Heavenly Father is not content with superficial emotion. And nowhere does love get such a strenuous test as in families. Families share limited resources, from apple pie to bathroom time. Because of their many years together, family members are often presensitized to faults and behavior patterns in one another. We ask each other, Why do you always squeeze the toothpaste from the middle? Why can't you ever remember to put away your dirty socks? And we share our hardest times.

What better testing ground could there be for love than the family? And what better example could there be for love than the Father? Father loves. Love is his name.

But love is a tricky business. We instinctively think that love is a feeling of fondness or affection. But even the best of earthly parents don't always feel fondly toward their children. Love is something more than a feeling of fondness.

Parental love is a commitment to always do what is best for the child. That is hard for humans. We tend to get in our own way.

I think of a friend I was visiting. We were standing in the entrance to his garage. As we spoke, his young son rode into the garage on his bike and parked it in front of their old station wagon. The father interrupted our conversation to stomp over to his son, grab him, hold him up in the air, and start to yell: "Why do you always—Why can't you ever—Won't you ever learn— What is it going to take—"

Let's leave our parental perspective and see the situation from the child's view. What do you think the son was thinking as he was suspended in midair with an angry face yelling his faults? Do you think he was saying to himself, "I am so glad that Dad is bringing these things to my attention. This will really help me"?

I don't think so. I don't think the boy was doing any quiet reflecting. I suspect that he was mostly feeling fear. Anger. Humiliation. Hurt. If my discernment is correct, the boy was submissive on the outside but hurt and angry on the inside.

When the father had finished his harangue, he paused, still panting from the angry lecture. Then he bellowed: "I love you." He set his son down and returned to pick up the conversation with me.

Again, let's take the child's perspective. Do you think the boy felt loved? I don't. I think he was hurt. The person who should be his friend, protector, teacher, and advocate had acted in total disregard for him. The father had expressed his own anger. But he had not acted in his son's best interest.

It is very characteristic of humans to be wrapped up in meeting our own needs and to be unaware of or insensitive to the needs of others. But Heavenly Father wants us to become more like him, always mindful of the needs of others.

Love is much more than saying, "I love you." If our children are to feel loved, our behavior must be responsive to their needs. Think of Elijah's experience. Three times the Lord listened to Elijah's complaint. Three times he did not lecture. But, when Elijah was prepared, the Lord taught him a great object lesson with wind, earthquake, and fire. It was because of the Lord's utter calmness that Elijah was able to feel the contrast when the Spirit spoke. If the Lord had yelled a brilliant lecture about duty and power, Elijah would not have learned the vital lessons.

As researchers on moral development have observed, when we use power and anger with our children, they remember only their own fear and hurt. When we calmly reason with them and point them toward consideration of others, they learn the reasons for expected behavior, they learn how their behavior affects others, and they learn to think in mature ways. They learn that the people who love them want to help them. Those are important lessons.

But every mortal parent gets angry. Every earthly parent gives lectures. Is it reasonable to ask parents to be so calm, serene, sensible? What can we learn from Heavenly Father about how to show love to our children?

The first lesson from Father about love may be to make time. That may seem quite easy for an eternal being. We mortals must use our creativity to find time for our children.

I remember when Andy caught me one evening just as I was dashing off to a Church meeting. He told me that his leg hurt. It had hurt all day. He thought something might be very wrong with it. He wanted me to help him. I wanted to be a good dad, but I had to go to a meeting. I was tempted to dismiss his pain: "It'll get better. It's probably just growing pains. You'll be okay." I even thought about judging him: "Andy, don't complain so much. We took you to the doctor when you had chest pains, and it was nothing." But I knew those approaches would not help. I felt trapped. In desperation I suggested: "Andy, I am going to a meeting. It will not go late. May I pick you up after the meeting? We will go out for dessert and talk about it. Is that all right?" Andy readily agreed. So, after the meeting I dashed home and picked up Andy, and we went to a restaurant. We ate and played tic-tac-toe on the paper place mats. We talked. And his leg didn't hurt anymore.

When we love someone, we make time for them.

The second lesson from the Father's example of loving is that he listens. He does not prepare his retort as we talk. He does not argue about our logic or about the facts of the case. He just listens. And he waits until we have gotten it all out.

Listening is a very great gift of love. And when we add gentle understanding, the gift is celestial.

I think of the boy who arrived home from school sullen and angry. When his mother asked him what was wrong, he insisted nothing was. Later his mother tried again: "You seem upset, son." The son glowered, then exploded: "On the way home from school the bus driver yelled at me, blamed me for stuff I didn't do, and called me names."

What would be your reaction if the boy were your son? Usually parents have one of two reactions. They vow to harm the bus driver: "He has no right to treat you that way! Get the bazooka and we will go down to the bus driver's house for a little discussion." Or parents blame the child: "I know you. You are a troublemaker. What did you do to provoke that poor bus driver?" Either response blames. Neither helps. The son has just expressed anger and pain over his humiliation. He needs healing understanding. "Ouch, son. It must have hurt to be humiliated in front of your friends. You probably felt embarrassed and angry." The willingness "to mourn with those that mourn; yea, and comfort those that stand in need of comfort" is the way that we "stand as witnesses of God at all times and in all things, and in all places" (Mosiah 18:9). Heavenly Father comforts. He invites us to do the same.

Some parents worry that such understanding may seem to endorse the son's behavior. "What if he really was a troublemaker on the bus? He needs to be accountable for his behavior."

Accountability is a true principle. So is compassion. There is a way to reconcile the two. First we listen, understand, and mourn with him. This sends a clear message: "I care about your feelings. I want to understand. You are important to me." *After* that message has been understood, after the boy feels peaceful again, then a sensitive parent may say, "Son, that was a very hard experience. Can you think of anything you can do to be sure it doesn't happen again?" Maybe he needs to sit with different friends on the bus. Maybe he needs to avoid certain behaviors that annoy the driver. Maybe he needs to talk to the driver about bus-riding expectations. The boy probably can think of very wise and sensible ways to prevent further trouble. But before he can get to solutions, healing needs to take place. And the wise parent heals with understanding. (If you want to be an expert at understanding, I recommend that you read Haim G. Ginott's *Between Parent and Child* [New York: Macmillan Publishing Co., 1965] or *Between Parent and Teen* [New York: Avon Books, 1969]. Ginott is the master of understanding!)

Have you ever been overwhelmed with pain? Have you ever found a place alone to weep with exhaustion and discouragement? And have you ever felt the warm glow of the divine presence accompany your grief? The message is that the heavenly hosts suffer with you as you struggle with the pain of a telestial world. Even Heavenly Father weeps to see us suffer. I have felt his understanding and compassion. I am thankful for his compassionate listening.

The third way that Heavenly Father shows us love is by customizing messages to our unique natures. He customizes his message to our style. He speaks to each person in his or her own language.

Scott is looking for peace and insight. Heavenly Father gives him peace and insight. Nancy is looking for opportunities to serve. Heavenly Father gives her beloved friends who need her. Wally is looking for joy. Joy is what he consistently finds. "Every man heard them speak in his own language" (Acts 2:6).

In this world most people exchange messages of love by some combination of three methods: telling, showing, touching. For some people it is critically important to hear the words, "I love you." Some people feel loved most strongly when someone does something for them—whether doing the dishes or helping with a lesson. There are people who love to cuddle, hold hands, be close. With our family members, we may learn to know and use the language that communicates love to them.

How can we design messages for each of our children that will be more effective in conveying our love? We can ask them what things help them feel loved. We can also notice those things that seem to be most effective. For each child the language is different. We can follow Heavenly Father's example and customize our messages of love for each of our children.

Fourth, because of the Father's love, he sees beyond our mistakes. When Moses refused to believe that the Lord could fill his mouth, the Lord did not demote Moses. He gave him Aaron. Even after Peter had been so shamefully irresolute, the Lord drew him up to lead the ancient church.

Some parents worry about spoiling their children with too much love. I suspect that no one was ever spoiled by too much love. Love is different from indulgence. Brigham Young provided an insightful balance: "I believe in indulging children, in a reasonable way. If the little girls want dolls, shall they have them? Yes. But must they be taken to the dressmaker's to be dressed? No. Let the girls learn to cut and sew the clothing for their dolls, and in a few years they will know how to make a dress for themselves and others. Let the little boys have tools, and let them make their sleds, little wagons, etc., and when they grow up, they are acquainted with the use of tools and can build a carriage, a house, or anything else." (*Discourses of Brigham Young*, sel. John A. Widtsoe [Salt Lake City: Deseret Book Co., 1978], p. 210.)

When our children have wanted to cultivate a hobby, we have supported them with time, encouragement, and resources. When possible, we provide the tools rather than the toys.

There are times when being loving is especially hard. Nancy and I learned a powerful lesson about love with one of our teenage foster children. She argued with us regularly. She lied to us often. We repeatedly felt irritated with her, which made it very hard to react to her helpfully. But we learned that, even when we were irritated, we could ask ourselves, "What would we do if we really loved her?" We learned to act with gracious concern even when we did not feel it. That helped us make kinder, wiser decisions in our relationships with her.

Taking time, listening, customizing messages, and seeing beyond mistakes are vital ways that we show our love for our children. But ultimately there is a higher kind of love. It is called charity, the pure love of Christ. It is a gift, a divine gift. Joseph Smith said that a person "filled with the love of God, is not content with blessing his family alone but ranges through the world, anxious to bless the whole of the human family" (*The Personal Writings of Joseph Smith*, comp. Dean C. Jessee [Salt Lake City: Deseret Book Co., 1984], p. 481).

Maybe charity is not possible for mere mortals. It is the Lord's love. And we only have such love when we are filled with his Spirit. As the hymn says, "*As I have loved you,* love one another" (*Hymns,* no. 308). Filled with his Spirit, we love as he loves. That is the state for which we are working. We are striving, even in this mortal world, to be filled with his Spirit so that we may love as he loves. We are striving to transcend the natural, mortal ways.

Family is a great testing ground. We may learn the fundamentals of love in our families. But it may stretch us beyond our mortal ability to love. It may stretch us to love as he loves. That is a joyous prospect.

Thirteen

GUIDANCE IS BETTER
THAN PUNISHMENT

And he did exhort them then with all the feeling
of a tender parent.
—1 Nephi 8:37

The Duke of Windsor said, "The thing that impresses me most about America is the way parents obey their children" (in Laurence J. Peter, comp., *Peter's Quotations* [New York: William Morrow and Co., 1977], p. 78). We don't want to spank our children, but we don't know how to get them to obey. Often it seems that there is no effective way to guide children. Guidance can be a source of immense frustration. It hardly seems to be an arena for joy.

When we think of discipline, we commonly think of threats and punishment. Those may be the most common ways that parents deal with their children's misbehavior. But they are not the best ways.

What is wrong with threats and punishment? One thing that is wrong with them is that they teach children bad things.

Consider threats. It is common for parents to get frustrated with their children and yell at them. "If you do that one more time, I'm going to whip you, young man!" "I've told you a thousand times. If I have to tell you once more—" Threats are bad because they insult children. They are likely to make the child feel dumb and put down.

There is something in every eternal soul that says: "No one has the right to insult me." Even discouraged children sense that it is not right to be treated as dirt. Threats are also bad because they may tell the children that we yell a lot but we never do anything.

Consider the mother who was loading her several little children into the car to go to the store. Just as she got them all in the car, the neighbor came over to talk to her. As the two ladies talked, the children became restless. One of the boys began to climb out the car window. The mother yelled for him to get back in the car. Then she returned to talking with the neighbor. Did the boy get back in the car? No. He continued to climb out the window. A few minutes later the mother turned and yelled again for him to get back in the car and threatened to spank him. He sat still while his mother yelled at him, but as soon as she returned to talking, he climbed out the window onto the hood of the car. When the mother spotted the boy on the hood, she yelled, "I have told you for the last time." Still she did nothing.

This boy had learned that parents yell a lot but do not really mean what they say. Threats insult children, but they do not teach them.

It is common for parents to nag. "Don't touch that!" "Leave her alone." "Go away." "How many times do I have to tell you?" Threats do not teach children to behave. They only teach children to resent insulting parents.

There are also problems with punishment. What does spanking teach a child? For many children it teaches that the world is a cruel place. It may also teach them that parents are mean. It may teach them that it is all right for big people to hurt little people. Not very good lessons. Trying to make children sorry for their mistakes through hurting them probably teaches all the wrong lessons. The most effective parents rarely or never use spanking.

There is something better than making children suffer. It is guidance. It includes structuring a safe, caring world and teaching eternal principles. We want to teach our children that rules are important, that people can work together and solve problems without being violent. There are several keys to successful guidance.

1. *Be careful about the rules you make.* Sometimes parents make too many rules. For instance, the lady who yelled at her children to stay in the car while she talked to the neighbor might have been wiser to talk to the neighbor later or to give the children something to do while she talked or to let the children play for a few minutes on the lawn until she was really ready to go.

Those would have been better rules than just asking the children to sit still while she talked.

Another place where parents have trouble is the grocery store. Most parents and children are tired and frustrated as they enter the store. Mom may ask her one-year-old to sit in the cart, be quiet, and not touch anything while she shops. Is that reasonable? Or would it be more reasonable to provide the child a toy to play with? Or to talk with the child or to give the child a box of animal cookies to eat or let the child hold purchases that will not get broken as he or she sits in the cart? The child may enjoy holding the broccoli and talking about it as Mother selects other items. An older child may be sent to get the vitamin pills or corn flakes for the family.

Parents sometimes ask their children to sit quietly with nothing to do in long meetings. That is not a reasonable expectation of little children. Maybe a child could play with a doll or a quiet book or a coloring book.

If we make rules that respect children's needs, they are more likely to learn to respect rules and to see the world as a safe, sensible place.

Sometimes the best rules are a result of a discussion between the parent and the child. A parent might say to the child: "I am very frustrated that you don't take care of the dishes right after dinner. What do you suggest?" The parent and child might work on the rule together until they agree. It might be that the child should be allowed to do some chore other than dishes. It may be that their favorite television show comes on right after dinner, and they should be allowed to watch television for thirty minutes before doing the dishes. If you cannot agree on a rule, the parent may have to say, "Let's go by my rule until we can think of a better one."

Being careful about the rules we make does not mean that we should not make rules. It means that rules should be reasonable. They should be adapted to the personality and age of the child. They should set up the child for success.

When our fourteen-year-old daughter, Emily, wanted to go to a high school dance, we felt that, as a junior high student, she was too young. We proposed that she have a party with her friends at our house instead of going to the dance. She thought it was a dumb idea. We suggested a movie or miniature golf. But she didn't like those any better. We invited her to come up with an idea that she felt good about and that we felt good about. She couldn't think of a better idea so she had the party at our house. She and her friends had a great time.

Our guiding principle is that it is our job to help each child get what they want in a way that we feel good about. We can help Emily have the fun with her friends that she wants without letting her go to a dance that we don't feel good about.

Do you have too many rules that are carelessly made and carelessly enforced? The start of good discipline is to make rules that are sensitive to the needs of children and allow them to grow as they should.

2. *Enforce rules consistently.* I remember hearing a mother tell her boy to stop picking at the cake that was on the table. But he kept picking. She kept shouting. He kept picking. She kept shouting.

When parents make rules that they don't enforce, children get the idea that we are not serious about rules. The mother might have been wiser not to leave the cake on the table in view of a hungry child. She could have gotten the child busy helping her. Or she might have cut a piece of cake for the hungry child. But if she asked the child to leave the cake alone and he did not, she might move the cake to the cupboard and distract the child with a different activity.

Being consistent in enforcing rules does not mean that the parent cannot adapt to circumstances. We make allowances for tiredness, age, influence of other children, and other factors. Consistency means that when we make a rule that we think is reasonable and a child violates that rule, the child would normally experience the promised result.

We observed a mother at the grocery store whose children would whine and cry for candy. She yelled, "I will not buy you candy!" But, as we were checking out, we noticed that her children were munching candy bars. She looked sheepish and muttered, "It was just easier than fighting with them." Then maybe the rule should be: If you help me with shopping, I will buy you one regular-size candy bar when we finish. Our family rule was: We will never buy you a candy bar to be eaten at the store. However, we will buy you animal cookies that you can eat as we shop. We will pay for them as we leave. Our children knew that we were serious about the rule. We did not nag them. But we tried to be sensitive to their hunger.

3. *Use consequences.* Consequences are different from punishment. Punishment hurts children. It makes them angry. Consequences teach children. They show the child that when he or she does certain things, certain things will happen.

In my family, each of our children has responsibilities. For example, they are expected to take their dirty clothes to the laundry room. If they don't get their clothes to the laundry room, they will not have clean clothes. That is a consequence.

Emily had a hard time getting up on time for school. We were always shouting at her and threatening her. Finally we bought her an alarm clock and told her that if she missed the bus she would be walking to school. She immediately became very good at getting herself up on time.

Sometime parents get into a contest of wills with their children. For example, Mother may say, "You may not go out and play until you have picked up your toys." By standing forbiddingly in front of the door, Mom may be saying to the child, "Let's see whose resolve is greater: my resolve to force you to clean up the toys, or your resolve not to be insulted." No one wins such a confrontation. Mom might say, "Before you go outside, we need to pick up your toys. May I help you get started?" Notice that this approach emphasizes cooperation rather than confrontation. It helps the child get started. If the child does not get started with putting the toys away even with Mom's help, the wise parent may pull the child close and say, "Are you feeling tired?" Maybe the child needs nurturing. Or maybe the child needs tickling to get the spirit of fun and energy going. The wise parent will be sensitive to the mood and needs of the child.

Consequences must not be used when a child is in danger. It is not appropriate to teach children the dangers of a hot stove or of busy traffic by allowing them to touch the stove or wander into traffic.

In many things my wife and I allow our children to follow their own preferences. We like our house tidy. Our son likes a "busy" room. We finally decided that the reasonable consequence for a messy room is for him to have a messy room. We let him live with the mess. We close his door if it drives us crazy. Once in a while we make a special request that he clean it up.

Using consequences can take a lot of wisdom. The objective is to allow children to see how their choices affect their lives. Consequences should not be used to punish. Learning how to use consequences appropriately is a very important and difficult skill.

4. *Give children real choices.* Tommy, the son of some friends of mine, was sitting on my lap as I read a book to him. After we had read for a while, he seemed to become bored. He got a pencil and looked like he was going to write in the book. His dad, who was in the room, noticed this and jumped at him, grabbed the pencil, and shouted, "You do not write in books!" I think it would have been more helpful to give Tommy a choice. His father could ask him: "Would you like to draw? We don't draw in books, but I can get you some paper to draw on. Or would you like to finish the book?" Either choice would have been fine.

Sometimes children resist us because we try to force them to do things. When we do not give them choices, they are more likely to rebel. A young child may resist going to bed. We may try to force the child. But they can resist us with calls for water and a light and a story. It may help to give choices. We might ask "Would you like Daddy or Mommy to tuck you in?" "Would you like to pick a storybook for me to read to you, or would you like me to pick one?" If the child says that he or she does not want to go to bed, we can ask the same question. The child has a choice within boundaries set by the parents.

We should give children choices only when we feel that either choice is acceptable. We do not let a small child decide to play with knives. Adult wisdom should frame choices for children.

5. *Keep it positive.* Sometimes children act up because they want us to notice them. They are especially likely to act up for attention if it seems that acting up is the only way they can get attention.

A father called me whose toddler was always whining and pulling on his pant leg. The father would get angry because it seemed that his little boy always wanted his attention. The father was afraid of teaching the boy to whine by responding to his whining. My question to him was, What is the boy trying to tell you with his whining? Maybe he is hungry, lonely, or tired. When we respond to children's needs, they are likely to whine less, unless they find out that whining is the only way they can get our attention. Then they will whine and whine. This father found that by taking more time for his son, the whining almost disappeared.

Sometimes we get so caught up in enforcing our rules that we forget about the relationship. Gwen could not get Melissa to take her nap. Sometimes she would yell at her or lock her in her room to get her to take a nap. But that only made Melissa angry. Gwen felt bad about the conflict she and her daughter were having about naps. Gwen found that she could read Melissa a story or start her watching a movie on TV. Melissa would fall asleep without any battle. Or Gwen could ask her to play quietly on her bed during rest time.

This wise mother learned how to get her daughter to take a rest without fighting with her. A mother should also be sensitive to the age at which a child no longer needs to take a nap.

Distracting a child can also be a very useful way to redirect the child. Tommy was playing on the floor with the pans and making a lot of noise. Normally Mother could stand the noise. But one day it was driving her crazy. Rather than jerk the pans away from Tommy and yell at him, she got out the play dough, went to the table, and started to make things with it. He became interested in the play dough and left the pans. That wise mother understood the power of distraction!

One of my favorite examples of guidance involves a mother and her two boys. After church the boys got into a fight that escalated until the younger boy swore at and attacked his brother. Mother was dismayed and angry with her son's behavior. She wasn't sure she was ready to handle it sensibly. So, when they got home she asked her son to go to his room to think about what happened. She went to her room to settle down and sort out her thoughts. After a while she went to the younger boy's room and said, "Son, I'm amazed and sad that you would act that way and use that language. I wonder if you understand some of the things that you said." She patiently explained how some of the words he used relate to sacred or grotesque matters. "It is offensive to God and to our family values for you to speak and act that way," she said. "Let me give you a choice. You could be grounded for a week for your behavior, or, if you are ready to repent you could apologize to your Heavenly Father and your brother." The boy was humbled and was glad for a chance to make amends. He knelt by his bedside to ask forgiveness of his Father. And he went with his mother to apologize to his brother. And his mother wrapped him in the arms of her love. (If the boy had not been willing to apologize, he still could have taken the grounding. Apologies should never be forced.)

This mother taught her son about an eternal pattern. He felt pain for his mistakes. He worked to make amends. Teaching this eternal pattern is what guidance is all about. As our children learn from our example and teachings to be wise and considerate, we discover that guidance can be joyous.

Fourteen

A RELATIONSHIP OF LOVE

*Can a woman forget her sucking child, that she should not
have compassion on the son of her womb?
Yea, they may forget, yet will I not forget thee.
Behold, I have graven thee upon the palms of my hands.*
—Isaiah 49:15–16

Children need more than love. They need continuing relationships with the people who love them.

People used to talk a lot about quality time with their children. But that seemed to mean, "I'm going to do something very nice and maybe even spend some money on you. But I only have half an hour, so enjoy it!" That is no way to build a relationship.

When I was a high school teacher, one of my students came to me after class and told me how he loved to go up to a nearby reservoir, crawl through the marsh, and watch the ducks. He asked if I would like to join him at 6 A.M. on Saturday. That time on Saturday morning is usually pretty committed for me. (Sleep!) But I thought it might be interesting. And I was pleased that the student would invite me to join him. At the appointed time we went and watched the ducks. I enjoyed it. A few weeks later the same student came to visit again. He told me that his father had arranged to take him big-game hunting. He had arranged a lodge, a guide, and horses. My reaction was, "Wow! Big bucks! I guess you are excited!"

The student thought for a long time. Then he mused, "Not really. I wish my dad would go with me to watch the ducks."

Relationships include taking time to be with each other. They are also about sensing the other person's unique hopes and wishes.

When little Andy came to me one evening while I was reading the paper and asked if I would take a walk around the block with him, I gave my stock response. "Not now. I am busy. I will later." Andy is gentle but wise: "Dad, you always say that." I was caught. I wanted to be a good dad. But I didn't want to waste any time! (Ouch!) Reluctantly I agreed to join him. I headed out the front door and around the block. Andy sauntered along looking at neat sticks and plants and rocks. I was champing at the bit and finally called out, "Andy! Come on! We've got to get around the block!"

Relationships are not built while running a stopwatch. They grow when people take time to be together. But there is more at issue than time. We need to be in tune with the other person's needs, feelings, preferences. Sometimes the opportunity to show our love comes at inopportune times and in unexpected ways.

When Andy got his Eagle Scout award, I offered to take him to a nice restaurant for dinner. He commented, "I don't know if that is what I want." I reacted, "I don't know if you get to pick what you get!" Later I repented and asked, "If you could pick what you got for your Eagle award, what would it be?" He replied, "Dad, I love to ski, but I don't have any skis. Could we go to yard sales and find some used skis for me?" It was a reasonable request. And I found some other excuse to go to that favorite restaurant. Now, I wish I could go back and cherish every childish moment with my beloved son!

For each person there is a different pattern of hopes, dreams, needs, and preferences. The hard part about building relationships is that we must be sensitive to the unique hopes and wishes of the person with whom we would be close.

If I buy Nancy a new dress and flowers, she will be polite. But she would rather that I keep her company, weed the garden with her, listen to her, and help her with the Relief Society newsletter. I tend to buy her things because that is the language that I understand. But it is not her language. I have to work to speak in her language. When I make the effort to communicate my love to her in her language, we connect joyously.

Each of us builds relationships in a different way. My daughter Sara wants me to be with her and laugh with her but not be embarrassing when her friends are around. My daughter Emily is at college. She wants us to honor our weekly phone time by listening, understanding, and loving. (She also likes us to occasionally send caramel popcorn.)

But what if we don't know how to show love to a given child? James Smith, a colleague of mine at Auburn University, has said that every child wears a banner. On that banner he or she tells us how much time, attention, control, and love they need. We can read those banners. Unfortunately they are not written in English. They are written in behavior. Our children tell us with their actions what they need.

If there is a universal formula of love, it probably includes taking time and being understanding. Taking time means doing things that our loved ones want to do. Understanding with our hearts means bringing to bear our pain and struggles and joys to understand how hard and joyous things can be for another person. Standing in mute respect, we can consider how others might be struggling in their own lives.

Sometimes our efforts at understanding show disrespect. When my dear colleague tells me that she has cancer and doesn't know if she will live and who will take care of her little girl, I might answer, "I know just how you feel."

But I don't know! I can't know! Instead I can invite her to tell me about her struggles. I can try to imagine how hard it is. I can say, "I probably cannot guess how frightening it is. But I am trying. Because I care." I can hug her. And I can cry with her.

We can cry with a child who has lost a valued doll. We can listen when our son is hurt by cruel comments at school. We can be patient and offer a dishcloth when our two-year-old spills her milk again. We can accompany a little one to the nursery when she is not quite ready to go alone.

Haim G. Ginott told about a Puerto Rican girl who struggled to read a passage to her school class. She struggled and stumbled. She finally quit and covered her face with her book. A kind teacher understood and said, "Reading English aloud is not easy. There is fear of making mistakes and of being laughed at. It takes courage to stand up and read. Thank you, Ramona, for trying." (*Teacher and Child* [New York: Macmillan Publishing Co.,

1972], p. 249.) Ramona's teacher understood her struggle and gave her courage to try again.

Mrs. Rhea Bailey was my fifth-grade teacher. She seemed to value me as a student. And I loved her for it. On the last day of fifth grade, she gave me a sealed manila envelope and asked me to take it home and open it with my parents. (Naturally I worried that she might have written a note to my parents about the time that I threw Sherry Lee Ball's sweater in the mud as an act of childish love.) I took the envelope home. I opened it with my parents. Mrs. Bailey had cut a circle out of construction paper and had written "Wally" on it. Then she had cut two narrow, ribbon-like pieces of paper and attached them to the circle so that it formed something like a state-fair ribbon. On each of the pieces of paper she had written a quality she thought she saw in me.

Do you think I threw away Mrs. Bailey's gift to me? Do you think I thought it was silly? Or do you think I saved it and it is still in my scrapbook? Thank you, Mrs. Bailey. Thank you for looking for and finding some good in a bashful, silly little boy.

Experts estimate that two-thirds of parents' interaction with young children is negative, including correcting, controlling, and punishing. When most of what children experience is negative, they may not feel that they have a loving relationship with their parents. But there are good ways to have fewer negatives and more positives in our relationships.

When Sara was very small, she observed one of our teenage foster children dusting items on the mantel. Sara was intrigued by the vase that was among those things. She asked her foster sister if she would hand her the vase. The automatic reaction was: "No! You're too little. You'll break it." Naturally this response did not satisfy Sara's interest in the vase. Sara found her mother in the kitchen. Nancy was not aware of the vase discussion between Sara and her foster sister. Once again Sara made her request to hold the vase. Nancy did several brilliant relationship-building things. First, she took Sara's hand as they headed into the living room and answered, "Sure, Sara. But did you know that vases are very breakable? Would you mind climbing up on the sofa, and I will bring the vase to you." (If we have the child stand on the rock hearth while we nervously watch her handle the vase, we are only setting her up for failure.) Sara was glad to sit on the sofa. Nancy got the vase and did another brilliant thing: she handed the vase to Sara so that she could feel its weight and texture. She had control of her experience. And Nancy did another relationship-building thing: she sat by Sara and talked with her about what she saw, about the markings on the vase, about what it meant to the family. When Sara had held the vase long enough, she said, "Thanks, Mom." And Nancy replied, "Sure, dear. If you ever want to see the vase again, just come and get me." What Nancy did was more than politeness. The net effect was to strengthen a relationship and to help a little person grow in her knowledge and confidence.

To build stronger relationships with their children, some parents schedule dates with their children. It may be for hiking or reading or shopping or cooking or sewing. What matters is that we take time for an activity that blesses both of us. Heavenly Father sets the example by inviting us to have an eternal relationship with him. He provided a Savior so that we might return and enjoy eternal life with him. Along the path he offers the warmth of the Comforter.

Just as we may feel safe and protected in the safe harbor of his love, so our children should feel safe and protected because they know that our "faithfulness is stronger than the cords of death" (D&C 121:44). Such a relationship requires effort and discernment, but it brings eternal dividends of joy.

Fifteen

TEACH THEM TO LISTEN
TO THE WHISPERINGS

And Samuel grew, and the Lord was with him,
and did let none of his words fall to the ground.
—1 Samuel 3:19

Our world is filled with loud, harsh, careless voices. The natural results are callousness, cynicism, and cruelty. Our world does not teach us to be sensitive to our quiet inner voices. Consider the terrible price we pay when we are educated by worldly voices rather than spiritual ones. We don't believe or trust or love. And we find it difficult to feel peace and joy.

There are at least two important ways to help our children be in tune with their inner voices. The first is to use discipline, guidance, and correction that encourage them to hear the inner voice. The Lord's counsel is: "No power or influence can or ought to be maintained by virtue of the priesthood [or, I would add, parenthood], only by persuasion, by long-suffering, by gentleness and meekness, and by love unfeigned; by kindness, and pure knowledge, which shall greatly enlarge the soul without hypocrisy, and without guile" (D&C 121: 41–42).

One evening we were watching television with friends. Good people. Gentle, loving parents. The mother was ironing while she watched the program. In the midst of ironing a dress, she turned to find that her four-year-old daughter was using the squirt bottle on a shirt that had already been ironed. The mother had had too much trouble from her very active daughter that day. She grabbed the squirt bottle from the girl and squirted her in the face while exploding with angry words of correction.

Was the mother "reproving betimes with sharpness, when moved upon by the Holy Ghost" (D&C 121:43)? It didn't feel like the Holy Ghost was behind her reaction. It sounded more like tiredness, anger, and frustration.

The mother's reaction was very normal. She was overloaded, and a thoughtless child had messed up her work. It was important to let the child know that her behavior was not helpful. It was also normal to feel angry. But it was not very helpful. Consider what the child learned from the interchange: Sometimes out of the clear blue, Mom goes crazy and hurts me. And I don't understand.

What was the mother to do? The mother might say to the child, "Honey, we don't spray the clothes after they are already ironed because it messes them up. But I would be glad to have you spray these clothes that have not been ironed. Here, would you spray the back of this dress?" The wise mother will do far more than teach the child what she should not do. She will teach the child what she can do to be helpful and will provide her with opportunities to serve and be busy.

One major issue between parents and children is power. Parents can use power to get the behavior they desire from their small children through threats, punishment, and force. But these methods work only as long as the parents are present (physically or psychologically) and have more power than the child. However, if you live by the sword you die by the sword. The child will not learn to be sensitive through harsh treatment. When there are loud voices of anger and indignation, it is hard to hear the inner voice. When children have more power than the parent or the parent is not present, they will act out their pain.

Researchers in the moral development of children have said that it is important to have the right amount of activation when we talk to children. For example, children can be underactivated. We may try to talk to them while they are watching television, and they don't hear a word we say. At the other extreme, we can become angry, shake them, and scream in their faces. They do not hear anything we say. They feel only fear and indignation. Consider an example.

Andy is very enthusiastic. That can scare a father when his son is running out of the house to jump in the car. So, time and again, I have asked him to slow down, be careful, and take driving seriously. His glib "Sure, Dad" did not bring me much comfort.

One night Andy found me in the kitchen and somberly announced, "We need to talk." My heart sank. We went to his room. He told me about driving around with his friends, acting silly, weaving between lanes, and accidentally cutting off a van. The driver was angry and followed him and took down his license number. Andy was expecting a squad of armed police to surround the house any minute.

I was relieved that nothing worse had happened. But I was also angry that Andy had been careless. I was angry that he had not taken my many warnings seriously. So I did what parents are trained to do: I preached. "Andy, what is wrong with you? Why can't you ever learn? How many times do I have to tell you?" I went on quite a while. I finally noticed that I was making myself sick. (I also should have noticed that my loud voice made it impossible for him to listen to his inner voice.) So I stopped. I asked if I might start over again. Andy wasn't sure if that was a good idea, but he submitted. I told him about the time when I was a high school senior and I was out driving around with my early-teen cousins, and they spotted a couple in love in the truck behind us. We started making fun of them. My cousins played like they were in love. I played with the blinkers. After a while it became clear that the fellow behind us did not think it was funny. So I turned off the highway. And I was dismayed to find that he followed us. I was dismayed to find that I was on a dead-end road. I was dismayed to find that, when I stopped at the end of the road, he parked right behind us. I was really dismayed to discover when he got out of his truck that he was wearing a university football jacket. But I thought I would be cool, just sit there and play like he wasn't there. He came to the side window and made me an offer: "Would you like me to break this window and drag you through it, or would you like to step out for me to beat you?" Two inviting options. I chose to step out. And he shared some thoughts and feelings with me that I still remember.

As I finished the story, I paused. "Andy, sometimes we learn lessons the hard way. But it is so important that we learn them."

Long silence. Finally Andy said, "Thanks, Dad."

"You're welcome, son. I love you."

When I was yelling and lecturing, any useful information was lost in the fury and anger. When I talked with Andy as a friend, we both learned.

Children need to know we are serious. But they also need to feel safe to listen and to feel understood. The optimal level of stimulation when we talk with our children is frequently found with a technique we call induction. Induction happens when a parent reasons with a child and explains the consequences for others of his or her behavior.

Let me give an example. Suppose that your son and his friends get caught late one night after using firecrackers to blow up the neighbor widow's milk box on her front porch. At the right time, when anger is not ruling reason, a wise parent might carry on a dialogue something like:

"It sounds as if you and your friends got carried away last night."

"Yeah, I guess."

"What do you think we need to do to make things right with Mrs. Jones?"

"Well, I guess we should fix her milk box."

"Yes. I agree. That's a good idea. I think that would help her a lot. What else might she need?"

"Uh, I don't know. We only blew up her milk box."

"Well, think about this with me. Mrs. Jones is a widow. She has lived alone for several years. I wonder if she sometimes feels afraid and helpless."

"I didn't think of that. But we weren't going to hurt her."

"Yes. Unfortunately she might not know that. How might she feel?"

"I guess she might have been frightened by the explosion and the commotion we made."

"Yes. She might have felt very afraid and vulnerable. Can you think of anything you and your friends can do to help Mrs. Jones deal with that fear?"

"We could go talk to her. Let her know that we are sorry. We really didn't want to hurt her."

"Good idea. I think visiting with her would help. It would be good for her to know that you did not intend to hurt her."

"We could also promise to look out for her and protect her from other kids."

You can see the critical elements of induction in the hypothetical dialogue: reasoning with a child and explaining the consequences for others of his or her behavior. A vital part of moral behavior is understanding the effects of our behavior on others by taking time to understand what others feel.

Using induction is different from sending a child on a guilt trip. It does not use blaming: "I can't believe you would—" "I thought you were a better person than to—" Instead, it teaches understanding and compassion.

Perhaps the latter days are a time when there are many loud and raucous voices. Loud music. Violent media. Cruel, mocking laughter. Flagrant profanity. Perhaps if our children are to survive turbulent times they must learn to be true to their inner voices of understanding, compassion, obedience, faith, and love. Our children must learn to listen to the inner voices in preference to the loud voices in the world.

The devil would have parents join the jarring, degrading, mean-spirited, accusing, dissonant cacophony of worldly voices. The Lord invites us to help children discover their own inner voices. Think about the parental behaviors that help children learn to listen to their inner voices. Calm reasoning. Gentle listening, like the Lord with Elijah at Horeb. Asking children how they feel about decisions. The scriptures perfectly describe attributes that can contribute to helpful parenting: persuasion, long-suffering, gentleness, meekness, and love.

Parents who want their children to learn the gentle language of the Spirit may choose not only to use gentler discipline but also for the family to watch less television, to choose gentler movies, and to make more time to be together in peaceful ways.

The second way to help our children be in tune with their inner voices is to actively help them learn the language of the Spirit. Not long before my mission, I remember going to a respected Sunday School teacher and asking how to get a testimony. People in the Church talked a lot about the Spirit. But it all made no sense to me. I had no idea what they were talking about. I was sure I had no testimony.

Ironically, at the same time that I was trying to get a testimony, I was having experiences of transcendent joy. But I did not recognize joy as related to God or his Spirit. For example, in my solitary work in the basement of a print shop I felt such overwhelming joy one day that I broke into exuberant hymns of praise. I sang and I laughed with joy. Several times my joy was so full that I retired to the rest room, where I was sure to be unseen as I knelt in prayer and thanked God for the consuming joy that I felt. But I wondered how to get a testimony.

About the same time in my life I remember visiting Temple Square with a new-convert friend from institute. I felt indescribable peace. It felt so good! Yet it was months later as Elder Harward and I knelt in earnest prayer for our struggling missionary contacts in Ocala, Florida, that I felt the same feeling and finally realized what it was: the Spirit of God.

How long and how many times the Holy Ghost may have tried to influence me before that time I do not know. I remember instances of transcendent joy. But I did not recognize the voice. I was still spiritually deaf.

We were spurred to a new tradition in our family one Sunday after a stake conference. As we sat at the dinner table, fifteen-year-old Emily began tentatively, "Today in stake conference when we stood to sing 'I Know That My Redeemer Lives,' I felt so happy that I cried. What does that mean?" Emily seemed to think there was something wrong with her.

Nancy and I rejoiced that she had heard that voice! We told her, "Emily, that is the Spirit of God speaking to your soul. The Spirit brings us comfort and teaches us new things, and sometimes we feel so good that we cry."

As a result of Emily's experience, we have developed a family tradition. Every Sunday at dinner we ask each family member (and any guests) if he or she would share the best experience of the day. It may be spiritual or not. Usually it is. Each of us tells how we were touched by a musical number, or the words of the sacrament prayer, or seeing a beloved friend. We want our children to notice the feelings that make life joyous. We want them to acknowledge the source. And we want to learn from each other's experiences.

One of my personal practices is to carry index cards to Sunday meetings. When the Spirit brings me a new insight, a deeper love, or sweet peace, I make a note of it. I don't want to get to the end of the day and be unable to account for the experiences of joy with which the Father punctuated my day. My kids tease me about the cards (and my bad memory). But it tells them how much I value his divine messages.

We also ask our children, when they are making decisions, how they spiritually feel about the issue. And we try to make our family relationships peaceful. We can express concerns to one another, but we try to be caring and respectful. We hope our children will become tuned to the gentle inner voices. Note the joyous promises God offers to those who cultivate the gentle language of heaven: "Then shall thy confidence wax strong in the presence of God; and the doctrine of the priesthood shall distil upon thy soul as the dews from heaven. The Holy Ghost shall be thy constant companion, and thy scepter an unchanging scepter of righteousness and truth; and thy dominion shall be an everlasting dominion, and without compulsory means it shall flow unto thee forever and ever." (D&C 121:45–46.)

Sixteen

TEACHING CHILDREN TO BE MORALLY CLEAN

Who shall ascend into the hill of the Lord?
or who shall stand in his holy place?
He that hath clean hands, and a pure heart.
—Psalm 24:3–4

Both parents and children dread the talk about human intimacy. We aren't sure how to convey two disparate messages: Intimacy with your covenant partner can be a wonderful and joyous experience. Intimacy is terribly wrong when it is experienced outside of marriage.

Those two messages could confuse anyone. Especially someone who is not trained in emotional subtleties.

Sometimes we attempt the plumbing lecture. We name the parts and tell about their functions as if directness and knowledge were the key. But anatomy is not the essence of intimacy.

Sometimes we try to instill fear: disease, pregnancy, interrupted education, shame, guilt, bad relationships. As adults we may forget that many teens live in a myth of invulnerability: "The boa might get *you*, but he won't get *me*." That is standard adolescent thinking. It takes us many years to discover that none of us is exempt from the penalties of law.

Sometimes we try to instill a heavenly vision of healthy relationships. Even so, the path of virtue is fraught with many practical challenges and dangerous hazards. The norms of the world as portrayed in hall chats at school and in the media is that you are weird if you are not doing it. Often. With many people. Further, it is a rare movie that does not glamorize and normalize casual sexuality. Movies can stimulate powerful desires that our youth do not know how to manage.

Teaching children to be morally clean takes more than talk—even wise, loving talk.

1. *The most important way to teach children moral cleanliness is to help them experience healthy, loving relationships.* Why should they save themselves for a celestial relationship if they do not believe that celestial relationships exist? Ideally our children should regularly witness a tender, growing relationship between their parents. Even in the absence of that, they should see love between generations: Mom can be friends with her mother, Dad can be loyal to his siblings, Uncle Jack can be a friend to the family.

Children should see loving relationships even if we need to arrange to go on picnics with the neighbors who model what we want our children to see.

Most important, our children should feel personally loved. Loved by us, their parents. Loved by a perfect Heavenly Father. I believe what Urie Bronfenbrenner said: "Every child should spend a substantial amount of time with somebody who's crazy about him or her. . . . There has to be at least one person who has an irrational involvement with that child, someone who thinks that kid is more important than other people's kids, someone who's in love with him or her, and whom he or she loves in return. . . . You can't pay a [person] to do what a [parent] will do for free." ("Nobody Home: The Erosion of the American Family," *Psychology Today,* May 1977.)

Think about each of your children. Does each of them have someone who is an advocate, a celebrator of that child? Every child needs that. It inoculates against bad relationship decisions as no other training can.

2. *Help your children develop on time.* Recently our school district proposed an AIDS curriculum that would teach fifth graders about the risks of unprotected sexual intercourse. There are undoubtedly some fifth graders in our school district who need that information. But they are not developing on a normal schedule.

To surround the whole understanding of human intimacy with fears about disease when youth do not yet understand the basics about intimacy is not wise. Those students who are ahead of schedule need help, but not at the expense of those who are on time.

Appropriate discussion topics for young children include the differences between men and women and the amazing process of reproduction. We have always kept a copy of *A Child Is Born* (Lennart Nilsson [New York: Delacorte Press, 1977]) on our bookshelf. When our children have had questions about how a baby develops, the answers can include amazing in utero photographs and a discussion of the miracle of life.

Parents can help their children choose and cultivate good relationships. When our children had friends who we did not prefer, we suggested that maybe they would like to have certain other friends over after school for cookies and games. With the help of teachers and visits to the classroom, we could suggest friends who seemed to share compatible interests, dispositions, and values.

There are very good reasons that Church leaders have encouraged youth to delay dating until they are sixteen. Children who start dating early are more likely to become sexually involved. They may also be forced into making decisions for which they have not adequately matured. They are expected to handle issues that are not developmentally appropriate.

But delaying dating until age sixteen is not the only guideline that is important. Even when our youth are sixteen, their dating should be of a friendship variety. Increasingly our teens want to be "going together." It takes wise, gentle, and patient parents to help children date in groups, with many partners, and in appropriate activities. In my family, our children are accustomed to discussing some basic issues with us before they go anywhere: Where are you going? With whom? What activities? What time will you return? They do not resist discussing these things with us because we have built a relationship of friendly involvement. We do not try to control, but we do stay involved and we do guide.

3. *Help your children learn to make good decisions.* We used to talk about self-esteem as the great cure-all. We now know that self-esteem cannot solve all the problems we expected it to solve. In fact, other characteristics may be far more important.

For example, self-efficacy. Self-efficacy is the feeling that we have control in our lives, that our decisions and behavior make a difference. It is clear that a child who is always told not to touch things, who has things grabbed from him, and who experiences no ability to make significant decisions as a child is not likely to develop a healthy sense of self-efficacy.

That is why agency is the bedrock of Heavenly Father's plan. Children should be given the opportunity to make decisions from the time they are small. But wise parents set up sensible choices. We do not ask our small children if they would like to stay up all night. But we might ask them at the appropriate time (they are tired and calmed) if they would like to be tucked into bed by Mommy or by Daddy.

Over the years, children should be allowed to make increasingly important decisions. A child may pick the flavor of Popsicles for the family. A school-age child may choose library books. An adolescent may help the family decide how to make family scripture study effective.

We can also give our children useful tools to use to help them get out of tough situations. We can teach them phrases to say such as, "Wow. My dad would kill me if I did that." "I think I will have a sneezing fit if I don't get some fresh air." We can also teach them how to redirect the situation toward something safer. When they are feeling pressured they might say, "Let's go get some ice cream," or suggest another activity.

4. *Help your children develop a clear standard embedded within strong values.* Our children sometimes get a confused message about standards: "You should not have intercourse before marriage. And you really shouldn't pet. So be careful."

What a setup for failure. Any normal person who kisses and embraces long enough with an attractive person will feel strong urges. Those urges are likely to express themselves in petting. After a couple have petted for a while, even stronger urges impel them toward intercourse—or any of the myriad intercourse substitutes that teens have invented to stay "safe" and "clean."

But such safety is about like having our teens line up along the edge of a cliff and trying to see how close to the edge they can stand without falling over. It is not a good game to play. It may be exciting, but it is very foolish.

Many attempts have been made at drawing a sensible line for chaste behavior. No petting. Or no intimate kissing. Or no extended kissing. But they tend to leave us looking silly and provincial while still leaving our teens playing an unwise game of sexual chicken.

There is a standard that makes sense. Elder Gene R. Cook has said that we do not have the right to stimulate or be stimulated by anyone who is not our spouse ("The Eternal Nature of the Law of Chastity," address, 1989, Ricks College, Rexburg, Idaho). I think that means that being turned on belongs to the marriage relationship. It should not be experienced by a dating couple. In fact, we should not be stimulated by books, movies, or flirting. Being turned on should be saved for the marriage relationship.

So, if kissing or daydreaming or dancing close or anything else outside of a marriage relationship is turning us on, it is wrong. An innocent kiss is an innocent kiss. But it is impossible to imagine innocent petting.

For males, there is a clear biological indication of stimulation. For girls, the measurement may be more difficult. But exactness and honor are necessary if we are to be truly clean.

We have had our children read the pamphlet titled *Is Kissing Sinful?* (Grant Von Harrison [Woods Cross, Utah: Publishers Book Sales, 1986].) Then we discuss it. We have concluded that a nonpassionate kiss may be appropriate if it is honest to the relationship. Intimacy does not belong outside of marriage. Even innocent affection does not belong outside a caring relationship.

5. *Help your children develop a compelling spiritual life.* Chapter fifteen in this book is about helping children learn to hear and heed the voice of the Spirit. Building a satisfying spiritual life is vital. Our children should experience religion as joyous! For example, family prayer is made meaningful when we unite our faith to bless people we care about. The sacrament is meaningful because it is a joyous renewal of our relationship with the Lord. Sacrament meetings are welcome because of the opportunity for genuine worship and fellowship.

A study by Latter-day Saint scholars on adolescent delinquency reports that "parents should recognize that it is important not only to hold home evening, family prayers, and scripture study, but also to seek ways to help their children to internalize

religious values by spiritual experiences" (Brent L. Top and
Bruce A. Chadwick, "The Power of the Word: Religion, Family,
Friends, and Delinquent Behavior of LDS Youth," *BYU Studies,*
Spring 1993, 33(2):308). It is not enough to go through the
motions. Our children need to feel the Spirit of the Lord acting
in their lives, inviting them to the profoundest joy.

Each of us finds certain spiritual activities more satisfying
than others. But all of us can experience Heavenly Father in our
lives. And our children should learn from us to rejoice in the
chance to know God.

6. *Be involved with your children.* There are ways to encourage
communication, and there are ways to kill it. We may, for instance,
demand that our children tell us what they have been doing. Such
an approach will almost guarantee that they will not tell us.

The scriptures remind us that "no power or influence can or
ought to be maintained by virtue of the priesthood [or parent-
hood], only by persuasion, by long-suffering, by gentleness and
meekness, and by love unfeigned" (D&C 121:41). Respect is not
demanded. It is earned by sensitivity, patience, and love.

Consistently we have asked our teenage children about their
dates. Consistently they have allowed or invited us into decision-
making with them. Some questions open doors: "How did you
feel about that date? What was the funnest part? What are the
qualities you enjoy most in the person? Is any part of your relationship confusing or frustrating? Do you feel that you are able
to have a fun, healthy relationship?"

Our questions have often been met with questions from our
children: "What should you look for in the person you date?
How is that different from what you want in a spouse? How can
I establish a friendship without feeling trapped or obligated?"

All parents make mistakes. But through our efforts to be interested, caring, and nondemanding, our children will learn to
lean on us for counsel.

When our children have wanted to date someone we don't
know, we invite that person over for cookies or kickball or dinner.
We do not cross-examine their dates. But we do get acquainted.
When our children are far away at school, we talk regularly on the
phone, asking them to tell us about their activities, dates, and
feelings.

Sometimes we express concerns. "Your romantic actions suggest that you are feeling like more than friends." "You seem to be making more emotional commitments than you realize." "Your behavior seems more serious than you have said that you want to be." We can help our children evaluate their feelings and their behavior.

One of the potential dangers of being involved with a teen's dating is that we might start to impose our own preferences. For us, there may be no good reason to go for ice cream after a dance that ends at midnight. But when we were teenagers, we probably thought there were good reasons. We may think that renting a tuxedo or buying a new dress is silly. But if they are willing to spend their own hard-earned money that way, it should be their decision.

In our family, when our children disagree with one of our recommendations, we invite them to make suggestions. Often they find a solution that we feel good about.

It is vitally important for parents to give their support and use their wisdom to help their children. Surveys are increasingly finding that teens are initiating sexual intercourse very early, even as early as eleven, twelve, or thirteen years of age. The preventive for this early sexual experience is clearly not more sex education in high school. It is wise and helpful involvement by parents. Parents should know where their children are, and they should know that they are appropriately supervised in appropriate activities.

7. *Help them establish a culture that supports healthy values.* We have some guidelines that govern decisions about our children's dating. The people they date must be earnest and good. The dates must involve wholesome activities. They must date several people at any one time rather than go steady with any one person until they are old enough for serious courtship.

We encourage our children to cultivate friendships with people of similar values. We gladly make our home available for their gatherings. And we try to make our home supportive of good values. We do not watch any movie without the recommendation of a trusted source. And our family does not watch R-rated movies. In fact, we have deliberately not hooked up our television to cable or to an antenna. We provide lots of good music and books, and we rent many classic movies.

The devil would have our children believe that all cool people are promiscuous and that their parents are hopelessly out of touch. How important it is for them to discover that good people take moral decisions seriously. There is much that parents can do to help their children take part with peers who are positive and whose activities are wholesome.

It should be clear that the parents' role in teaching their children to be morally clean goes far beyond the "talk." Children are more likely to be clean and good and earnest when we have a balanced program of growth for them. No parent is perfect. But we may do well by applying sensible principles, by maintaining loving relationships with them, and by calling upon the Father to help us. We can prepare our children to find joy in healthy intimacy.

Seventeen

FUN SPACES:
DESIGNING THE HOUSE
FOR FAMILY LIVING

Why not?
—Larry Austin

Think about your home, whether it is an apartment or manor house. Which rooms are used most by your family? Which are rarely used? In which rooms do you have the most confrontations with your children? ("Don't touch that. Get out of that room. You're making a mess!") Do you spend too much of your time cleaning the house? Is your house designed for your family? Do you need to redefine spaces in the house to better accommodate the family? Do you need to adapt your house to encourage family joy?

Ronald L. Molen (see *House, Plus Environment* [Salt Lake City: Olympus Publishing Co., 1974], pp. 41–46) has said that every home should have several kinds of places:

1. *A place to gather* where people can sit and chat comfortably. Maybe around a fireplace. Or a conversation pit. A place where family members naturally gather in order to relax and visit.

2. *A place to dine*—not just a bar where people grab their microwave dinners, but a place where the family can sit together for dinner and talk. Eating on the run or in front of the television leaves family members leading separate lives. Eating together can be a great time for sharing.

3. *A place to play and relax.* Children need a place where they can finger paint or create things with play dough without getting

into trouble. Children need a place where playing and creating is encouraged. Maybe there are murals or ladders, ropes, platforms, a fireman's pole. It can be a place that is colorful and fun.

When our children were small, we built a house with a great room with a vaulted ceiling that included the kitchen, dining area, living room, and office. Above the great room was a loft where we kept the children's toys, books, train, and games. They could build Lego castles or playhouses. But Mom and Dad didn't have to see the mess or step on stray Legos. Yet the children were close to us. We could talk to them while we cooked. They could tell us about their inventions. This design worked well with our young children. As our children entered the teen years they needed more distance, in part so that they could make their own kind of musical noise.

4. *A place to be alone.* Maybe it is a bedroom or quiet room where a child can read, think, study, build a model airplane, or do whatever else they want.

5. *A place to remember* might be an attic room, a dormer window, or a treehouse. A place for reading mysteries and adventure stories. A magical place that children will remember.

It is common for us to design houses according to tradition. A formal living room. And a family room. Maybe a game room. A library. A dining room with nice furniture, where no one ever dines. Such homes may impress the neighbors. But they are not very good for families and children. It is better to design a home that supports the activities and relationships that should develop there.

We have tried to develop places that were fun and memorable and fit the children's needs. We call them fun spaces.

When Emily was small, her bedroom in our older home had a dormer window where she liked to play with her dolls. We built a playhouse in the dormer where she could have her dolls. Above the playhouse was a sleeping loft that was accessed by stairs and railing. For Emily the place was magical.

In the yard of one of our homes, we had two tree houses. Between the two tree houses was a bucket trolley that allowed the kids to pass messages and Twinkies back and forth between the tree houses. From the lower tree house there extended a zip line.

The kids could jump out of the tree house holding to a rope and sitting on a board and zoom across the yard supported by a steel cable.

When Andy reached the age when he wanted an unusual room, we were restoring a historic home in rural Utah. His room was small but tall. We played with many ideas. Finally we settled on a western town theme. We replaced the door to the room with an old metal vault door that came from a building that was being razed. We built an Old West facade just the right distance from the wall to accommodate a double mattress. It included a reading loft with a bookshelf behind Dr. Aardvark's Snake Oil Emporium. On the lower level of Andy's Boarding House was his Lionel train. On the upper level was his bed, with a fireman's pole to slide down. There was also the Uintah State Bank with a hinged facade that allowed adults into the room without stooping. There were other details. Period light fixtures. Painted mesas on the wall. A rocking horse with a miniature leather saddle. Old West movie posters. It was a place where Andy and his friends could hide out from the evil sheriff (usually his dad), ride the train, and chase bad guys. It was a place to live dreams. The cost for the project was minimal because we built much of it with cast-off lumber and secondhand treasures.

Later, when we built a new house, Andy chose a different motif: camping out. We set up the family tent, which filled the room. We put a cot and sleeping bag in the tent. (Andy hated making his bed!) A ficus tree. And glow-in-the-dark stars on the ceiling. In his closet we cut a trapdoor into the crawl space for a hideaway. The cost was less than for traditional furniture. But Andy loved it.

And Sara wanted a special place. So for her we built a play-house fashioned after an English cottage. It was the perfect place for tea parties.

While in high school Andy wanted more room for his art studio. So he gave his queen-size bed to Sara and filled his room with his art table, books, and projects. He sleeps on a cushion on the floor.

We still have dreams to build a ship structure around one of the giant, mast-like trees in the yard of our home. The new zip line would be accessed from the crow's nest.

And we would like to build a miniature castle complete with towers, moat, and drawbridge. We keep files of castle pictures. We doodle. But our children are almost grown. Maybe we will build it for the grandchildren.

There are several principles we have learned in the process of our projects. Ingenuity is more important than money. It takes time and tenacity. We are kept young by our dreams. The best designs are sensitive to the needs and interests of the family members who use the space.

Your family may be less zany than ours. Maybe you like traditional designs. But maybe you also like joyous surprises. Maybe you like to design your spaces to fit your family. Maybe you want to encourage your family's talents and interests. Maybe you want your house to be fun.

Well, why not?

Eighteen

JOYOUS REMEMBRANCES

Having been highly favored of the Lord in all my days;
yea, having had a great knowledge of the goodness
and the mysteries of God, therefore I make a record
of my proceedings in my days.
—1 Nephi 1:1

Perhaps every experience in our lives is a gift from God. Some experiences bless us. Some humble us. Some comfort us. But all can teach us. Our lives are a gift from God.

Perhaps that is what family history is about: understanding, preserving, and celebrating God's gift of life. Yet any talk about family history generally arouses feelings akin to those felt when the opportunity of washing Thanksgiving dishes is announced: dread.

Perhaps that is because we have emphasized the doing without understanding the purpose. Some dutifully do it while hating it. Most of us choose not to do it and feel guilty about our neglect. The guilt is more bearable than the history.

What Mark Kunkel says may apply to family history: "Don't forget, this is supposed to be fun." Consider creative and potentially joyous ways that the job might be done.

1. *Preserving the day to day.* I have dedicated a drawer in my desk at home to saving special things. When a family member appears in the newspaper or when Sara makes me an angel in school or when one of the children submits a handwritten proposed compromise to break a family deadlock or when I get a letter from a dear friend, those cherished papers are dropped in the designated drawer with no more trouble than making sure that

they have a date and identifying information on them. At the end of the year I gather up the contents of the drawer and put them into a folder that I drop into the filing cabinet. For any year since I was born, I can go to the file to find cherished reminders of the lessons of the year.

There are faithful Latter-day Saints who keep a journal every day. My dear wife is one of them. But there are many who are not so faithful. Most of us buy a lovely journal with renewed resolve. We make a few entries. But soon the effort is crowded out by competing demands, and we are left with only tarnished dreams.

My solution is to keep a month-at-a-glance calendar. The calendar is not the wallet-size one in my pocket. It is a separate calendar that is about notebook-size. Though there is only a two-inch square for each day, that is just the right amount of space for me to record the major doings of the day. There is no room for detail. But if something extraordinary happens that needs more comment, I write it in the margin. Outlining each day's events generally takes less than a minute. And I have a code system for keeping track of the clearly recognized gifts from God: those times when I distinctly felt the Spirit of God, I place a "+". The size and character of the plus sign remind me of the power and nature of the experience. The process makes me more alert to heavenly messages.

Sundays are the days when Heavenly Father usually teaches me the most. I used to get to the end of the day and remember that I had felt especially blessed or enlightened, but I couldn't remember the ideas and thoughts. It seemed that I was an improvident student to be tutored by Father yet so quickly forget the lessons. So every day and especially on Sundays I carry index cards in my shirt pocket. When Heavenly Father warms and teaches me, I make a note. At the end of the day I can review the blessings of a kind and wise Father, and the cards are saved in a file. I don't know that the cards will ever be useful. But they are to me a reminder that life's experiences are sweet gifts from Father.

2. *Seeing a bigger picture in our lives.* A tiny outline of daily doings does not capture all the meaning of our lives, not even when we have thousands of little squares. The skeletal outlines

take on flesh when they are woven together in patterns. That may happen weekly when we sit down to write to parents, children at school, or dear friends. By saving a copy of our letters we bring our history to life.

It can also be satisfying to collect our related experiences into essays. I have been amazed at the systematic way that Heavenly Father has taught me when I look at experiences over the years. So I have written essays about helping the poor, coming to know Heavenly Father, finding hope, and overcoming prejudice. The essays may never be of interest to anyone. But for me they are a way of acknowledging the Father's continuing tutoring. I collect them as a reminder of what the Father is teaching me.

I don't write the letters or essays because it is required. I write them because they bring joy. Often it is hard to get started. But as I work to find the hand of God in my life and the lives of those I love, I am flooded with an enlarged sense of his goodness. Almost every week that I have sat down to write to missionary parents or missionary children, I have overflowed with joy in his goodness.

Maybe you express yourself in art or poems. My friend Phil is an artist. He adds delightful illustrations to his narrative. There are many ways to capture the joyous and challenging lessons of life.

3. *Connecting with our ancestors.* I was visiting with my Aunt Ruth one day when I commented casually how I wished that I had a photo of the old green cabin where Grandpa Goddard used to spend summer evenings with his family. In my childhood I had spent many magical days exploring in and around that cabin. It seemed impossible that such a picture should exist. But I craved the chance to connect my boyhood experiences of the cabin to my father's boyhood days at the cabin. Aunt Ruth told me that she could not remember ever seeing pictures of the cabin, but she did have a big box full of newspaper clippings and junk from Grandpa Goddard. Would I be interested in it?

It is funny how lovingly a person can welcome a messy accumulation of dust, yellowed newsprint, and miscellaneous scraps that Grandpa thought were too precious to discard but too mundane to feature in a scrapbook. So he dropped them in a box. When I got home I opened the box and started carefully sorting through its contents. There were broken parts of eyeglasses. There were many news clippings that were apparently saved because of Grandpa's interest in the subject. There were files of his correspondence. There were newspapers that were saved for no apparent reason—maybe he planned to read them later. All of them I lovingly sorted into piles.

And there were several brown envelopes that had once held photos. I looked through the accompanying negatives. Many were too dark to be usable. Some showed scenes from travels. And one envelope contained pictures of the family gathered together at the old mountain cabin.

What a gift! One photo shows my grandparents and great-grandparents together with my father (who was then a little boy) and his siblings gathered in front of the cabin. In another the family is relaxing by the stream behind the cabin. And in yet another the cabin is shot from a nearby hillside. How I cherish the connection that those photos provide me with my beloved ancestors!

The papers that once filled a cardboard box are now sorted into files. The most important documents, those that tell the story of Grandpa's life, are put in a special file in chronological order. It is a joyous blessing to sort through the papers that help me understand my beloved grandfather.

Because we lived near Nancy's grandparents for many years, our children were blessed by the loving care of their great-grandparents. They heard (and we recorded on tape!) Grandpa Thacker singing the chicken song and uncounted, delightful songs he sang as a child entertainer when singing was a welcome diversion from gnawing labor. In late life Grandpa started writing poems. Our lives were richly blessed by our visits, by his songs, poems, and stories. So we gathered up the cherished photos and typed up the poems and made copies for families and friends. It is expensive and challenging to make a book. But anyone can make a scrapbook in a three-ring binder. We are glad that each of our children has a scrapbook of Leslie Price Thacker to remind them of the tenacity and humor that they inherited from their great-grandfather.

Some forms of family history reside best in files and closets. But every home can be blessed by pictures and collectibles inherited from our ancestors. Some families even develop a heritage wall where they display pictures of ancestors. They may also make a section showing the joy of their own family doings.

Meaning can also come in meetings. I remember a family gathering when we met near the old, green cabin. Aunt Ruth stood by the fire pit and called dozens of Grandpa's descendants to order. When all had settled, she started: "Children, you need to know how we love you." I am not sure why I was so overwhelmed by the sweet joy of that testimony. But tears flooded my face as she told of the legacy of love that has blessed our lives.

I think Mark Kunkel was right: "This is supposed to be fun."

Nineteen

GIVING ALLOWANCES AND HEADING TO ZION

Impart of your substance to the poor.
—Mosiah 4:26

"But Dad, these shoes are worn out. And they hurt my feet."

"They look perfectly good to me. We only bought them last fall. Why, when I was your age—"

The battle for resources in families is familiar to most of us. We want our children to learn frugality and care. They want to be cool. So we are continually at odds.

Probably the most common pattern of allowances is to provide children some spending money in addition to providing for their basic needs. When I was a teenager, that meant that I was always frustrated with my parents for not buying me more and cooler clothes, while at the same time I expected to have almost unlimited spending money from allowance and part-time work for luxuries such as Beach Boy albums and movies. So I had the worst of all worlds: I did not learn frugality, and I was at odds with my parents. Worse yet, I was totally absorbed in my own needs.

Nancy and I reached a critical juncture with our children when Emily was a teenager. It did not seem right to always be at odds. So we decided to try a new program. With Emily and Andy we added up the annual cost of purchasing a *basic* wardrobe. One new pair of shoes. One pair of jeans. And so on. The amount was very conservative. We divided the amount by the fifty-two weeks of the year to determine the weekly amount.

Then we paid them that amount as allowance but made them fully responsible for purchasing their own clothes. The kids thought they were rich!

But they found that clothes can be expensive. Suddenly we were working together to find sales. Hand-me-downs became more attractive to them. Shoes were made to last longer. Clothes were bought more carefully.

There were still special challenges, such as when Sara wanted to go on a big trip with her school choir. It was expensive. We agreed to pay half. She paid her half with her allowance and earnings from baby-sitting. It was a real sacrifice on her part. But it helped her evaluate the benefits of the trip.

So we were working together, and our children were learning frugality. But there is more to learn about money. We also asked our children to always pay a full tithe. And to put half of all earnings (excluding their allowance) into savings. They have not always liked the idea of saving. But as Andy headed to college, then a mission, with four thousand dollars in the bank, it made sense to him. (Unfortunately Emily is much like her father: She can think of a dozen uses for every dollar she earns.)

There was still the holiday sinkhole. I remember the year that Nancy assigned me to buy presents for Andy's Christmas while she bought for the girls. I bought Legos. And mechanical kits. And electronic devices. I spent three hundred dollars on gifts for him but still wondered if I had bought Andy things he would enjoy. I learned that it is possible to make ourselves poor without blessing our children.

So we have developed a new holiday system. Now we designate a specific amount of money for each child's gifts. We let them decide how they want to spend it. The things they select are wrapped and put under the tree. In addition, we buy small gifts and stocking stuffers as fun surprises.

For children who still believe in Santa, the traditional system of trying to overhear children's requests on Santa's knee may be all right. But what our family's system for older children lacks in magic and enchantment, it makes up for with adult good sense.

But there is still another lesson to be taught about money: sharing with the poor. Hugh Nibley has acted as a Latter-day Saint conscience for a full generation. I was startled when I first read his "Work We Must, But the Lunch Is Free" (see *Approaching Zion* [Salt Lake City: Deseret Book Co., 1989], pp. 202–51). Nibley has reminded us that God expects us to be active and productive. And God will provide. But we do not need more stuff. We need to take care of one another. That is what Zion is about. That is what the gospel is about. "And the Lord called his people Zion, because they were of one heart and one mind, and dwelt in righteousness; and there was no poor among them" (Moses 7:18).

So when our children are planning their holiday requests, we remind them that they may choose to use some of their allocation as part of our effort to help a family in need. Of course, their allocation is so small that we do not expect that they will want to use any of it for someone else. But one Christmas Emily and Sara combined to buy a nice toy for a younger child. Andy bought a basketball backboard for an older child. Nancy and I bought gifts for the parents. Our children made the sacrifice gladly. I believe they enjoyed the presents they bought for others more than they enjoyed their own gifts.

I think of the time in my childhood when I had planned to get a coat for Christmas. But filled with the spirit of giving, I suggested to my parents that I keep my old coat and they use the money to help a poor family. Despite the fact that my parents are some of the most compassionate people on the face of the earth, they are also practical. They dissuaded me, saying, "Wally, you need a coat." I guess I did. (Maybe they had already bought the new coat.) But I still wonder if I might not have been warmer in my old coat with the knowledge that I had helped someone needy.

One November, as Andy's birthday was approaching, we asked him at the dinner table what he wanted for his birthday. He thought for a long time. (This is a boy who bought most of his wardrobe from a secondhand store.) Then he said, "I don't really need anything. Do you know a family that needs something?"

"Yes, we do," we replied. As a result of Andy's graciousness, there is now a struggling family that has the timing chain they needed for their car.

Our children also learn about the challenging and growth-promoting process of helping the poor by observing or hearing about our own struggles as parents. Some of our most challenging opportunities come when Nancy and I go to professional meetings in major cities. One such trip took us to New Orleans. Most of my time was spent in meetings. Much of Nancy's time was spent touring and reading. Through the week she kept asking me how we could help some homeless people. I felt irritated by my wife's persistence and by my own sense of helplessness. As our week of meetings was almost complete, Nancy put it directly: "I have most of my birthday money left. Let's go down in the morning and find someone to help." I liked the idea in principle. But when morning came and we were walking along Canal Street in pouring rain with clusters of homeless people in every merchant's doorway, the impossibility of our situation (and our naïveté) became painfully obvious. We walked back and forth several times before we finally just dove in. I walked up to three ragged, older men and asked if my wife and I could take them to breakfast. They were disbelieving but then jubilant. We tried to crowd the five of us under our umbrella to make our way around the corner to the closest eatery, a McDonald's. I invited them to step up to the counter and order anything they wanted for breakfast. I was surprised when they refused, saying, "Get us whatever you want to get us, and we will be happy." I coaxed them to make their wishes known. They took a booth. Nancy and I ordered breakfast for them and for us. As we ate, we asked about their lives and families. One told proudly of his children and grandchildren. He observed without complaint that he was not welcome in their homes. One told proudly of his Vietnam war service. Each had a story to tell. They seemed to glow in the warmth of our interest and appreciation. We extended breakfast as long as we were able. Nancy nodded to me. I knew what she wanted me to do. I divided the cash that Nancy had refused to spend on herself for her birthday among the three men. They were speechless. They had asked for nothing. It was clear that they wanted to embrace us. It felt good to hug them and consider how dearly Heavenly Father loves those lonely, hapless sons. We have saved the paper napkin on which they signed their names and wrote us messages.

But the breakfast outing had its complications. Another streetwise man had seen us pass with his peers. He asked to join us. He was very persistent. As we walked, he talked loudly of his hardship. He insisted on twenty dollars in cash. We offered to buy him breakfast. While the others waited in the booth, he ordered breakfast and insisted on money. When I offered him ten dollars he insisted on twenty. He cajoled, chanted, and wheedled. I held to my offer. Later, after breakfast was complete and all the men had left, the manager approached us and asked that we not bring problems into his business.

Our professional conference-going gives us an annual opportunity to try to be helpful in settings that are unfamiliar to us. We generally do not give out cash. We offer to buy a meal. It is common to worry about the inappropriate uses of money given to the poor. But we also consider King Benjamin's counsel: "And if ye judge the man who putteth up his petition to you for your substance that he perish not, and condemn him, how much more just will be your condemnation for withholding your substance, which doth not belong to you but to God, to whom also your life belongeth; and yet ye put up no petition, nor repent of the thing which thou hast done" (Mosiah 4:22).

We are aware that we go to his throne of grace as penniless beggars. We must keep trying to help one another if we expect to be rescued by his goodness.

Many opportunities come unexpectedly. When a college student counted out sixty-eight cents to the cashier for gas, we were able to quietly add five dollars to his purchase.

So we invite our children to join us in discussions about better ways to be helpful. Our children also participate directly in various efforts to help. When the Lions Club assigned me to deliver a check to a needy family at Christmastime, I invited Nancy and the children to help. We all bought little gifts. Emily made cards. Sara helped cook treats. And Andy (then about nine years old) dressed up as a miniature Santa. Once he had donned my big boots and his mother's big, red sweater and covered his face with cotton balls, he did not look like Andy. On the appointed evening little Andy Claus went to the door of the recipient family. They welcomed their little visitor with good humor. He handed out the presents. Then he handed the parents an envelope, wished them Merry Christmas, trundled down the walk, and joined me in hiding in the bushes across the street. It was only moments later that the mother came to the door screaming, "Santa! Santa! Come back!" It is not common for little Santas to leave $250 checks. The bulk of the gift was from the Lions Club. But it was a blessing for all of the family to participate in the tidings of Christmas joy together.

The kids also watch us strive to pay a generous fast offering. We invite them to be generous. They also watch us strive to serve in Church callings. We involve them as appropriate. And we encourage them to participate with us in church and community service projects.

It is important for kids to learn to be frugal. It is also vital for children to learn to be generous, "for God loveth a cheerful giver" (2 Corinthians 9:7). So much that is joyous and eternal as well as practical can be learned at home.

Twenty

FAMILY FUN AND TRADITIONS

It doesn't get any better than this.
—Andy Goddard

Dorothy Parker has said that "the best way to keep children home is to make the home atmosphere pleasant—and let the air out of the tires" (in Laurence J. Peter, comp., *Peter's Quotations* [New York: William Morrow and Co., 1977], p. 77). There are still other ways. The Lord has given us great traditions that help us to connect and relate to each other.

Proactive Parenting

The most basic tradition may be to enjoy each other. Child development researchers have observed that a very high percentage (between sixty and eighty percent) of the interactions between parents and their young children are negative. They involve forcing a child to do what the child does not want to do or preventing the child from doing what he or she is determined to do.

You know the script. A child wants to play with the remote control. You don't want him to break it or lose it. You try to pull it away. A fight ensues. That same kind of tug-of-war between parents and children can continue through lifetimes and generations.

But it doesn't have to. Wise parents plan ahead to make their interactions positive. With infants, that may entail child-proofing a house and becoming skillful in the art of distraction. With school-age children it may mean setting aside time after school for snacks, walks, and small talk. With teens, it may mean a willingness to be patient and understanding and also to pray for opportunities to connect meaningfully.

Making the Ordinary Fun

Healthy relationships are built on shared joy. But shared joy is not always programmed. It happens not only in planned vacations but also in the way we live with each other. Do we enjoy laughing and sharing at the dinner table? When we ride together in the car, do we talk and share? Do we make weeding the garden fun by joining in a spirit of teamwork, slam-dunking weeds into the wheelbarrow, talking to the weeds, sharing soft drinks?

Family Connections

When you were growing up, did you have a favorite relative? Some come immediately to my mind. On holidays, Uncle Jack would visit. He would laugh and chase us around the house and tickle us. We loved him for it.

And Uncle Grant. He would talk to us. He took us to his mine. He and Aunt Mary invited us to stay at their house. They had a gift for making the summers magical.

At family gatherings, Grandpa Goddard told us poems and limericks. He could go on for hours. How I love remembering his telling of "This is the domiciliary edifice erected by John," a unique version of "This is the house that Jack built."

And Grandma and Grandpa Wallace used to visit on Saturday afternoons. They would bring brown bags filled with treasures that a young family's budget could not allow: ice cream bars! breakfast cereal with toys inside!

Families can be strengthened by getting together and by sharing. No amount of holiday football can compensate for human connections. The principle is very basic: It feels good to be noticed by people you care about.

Continuity

A feeling of safety comes from continuity. The activities may be as simple as milk and toast for Sunday supper or going with Mom to the store or taking a ride with Dad. It may include getting your favorite candy bar in your Christmas stocking or having Dad call you by a silly nickname.

We used to get to watch Perry Mason with Mom and Dad on Saturday evenings. Once in a great while we got to go to Tampico with them for dinner! Going for a malt with Grandpa. Such simple little rituals make life enchanting.

Traditions

When two people marry, there is likely to be some struggle to have the new family adopt the traditions from each partner's family of origin. Years can be spent fighting about whose family should be visited at Christmas and how much the tooth fairy should give.

A wise couple will identify their values and carve new traditions based on their unique togetherness. For example, Nancy would be happy to have Christmas be a time to sit together for music and quiet talk. I favor lots of food, presents, and frivolity. But when Nancy and I examine our values, we find that we both want joyous togetherness with spiritual meaning.

So on Christmas Eve we have a Jerusalem dinner. Each of us dresses in a bathrobe with a towel wrapped around our head. By candlelight we eat olives, grape juice, pita bread, fish sticks, and Fig Newtons. (Not quite authentic Jerusalem fare, but close enough.) We gather around our life-size Nativity scene to sing together and retell the story of the Savior's birth. It is joyous and meaningful.

But Christmas morning, each of us has a stocking full of favorite junk food and little joys. Presents. Peanut butter cups. Enchiladas for lunch. There is one major Christmas morning concession to Nancy: the youngest family member distributes gifts one at a time, and we all watch as that person opens the present.

Traditions can be a burden or a joy. In some homes, family home evening only teaches children how frightfully long eternity can be when you are bored. We have tried to make home evening fun: Hymn. Invocation. Short lesson with stories. Questions and discussion according to their interest. Hymn. Family prayer. Treats!

Likewise, family prayer can be a dreaded and dreary interruption of life. Or it can be a time to talk with Heavenly Father. Occasionally we declare a family hug at the end of prayer. As we all wrap our arms around each other, we are likely to start swaying and laughing.

You can tell when your traditions are appropriately joyous by the children's willingness to remind you of them: "Mom, we haven't had family prayer yet."

Feeling of Magic

Sometimes families have a feeling of magic. Every few years our family would make the drive from Utah to Southern California, where we rented a beach house and went to Disneyland. Dad's struggling income and growing family made it a real sacrifice. But I still remember one particular evening as a child in a Travelodge along the way with my family. We sat in front of the TV and ate crackers and cheese. It seemed too good to be true! Motel room! Snacks! TV! Maybe when families try to give their children everything all the time, nothing is left to be magical.

The best family traditions tie us together in loving and joyous ways. As Andy said when Emily came home from college and we were gathered together for Nancy's delicious chicken tacos: "It doesn't get any better than this!"

Twenty-One

BIG LESSONS FROM
LITTLE BOOKS

That's silly. Bears are bears.
—Lars's father

What books do you remember from your childhood? Maybe Dick and Jane readers. Maybe *The Little Engine That Could.* Maybe *The Brave Little Tailor.* Maybe Nancy Drew mysteries. It depends on many things. But it is likely that the books of your childhood have affected the way you see the world.

For instance, most of us learned to chant "I think I can. I think I can. I think I can" from the story about the little engine that could. I have a friend who spent years in Thailand who says that they have essentially the same story there, except that the engine says, "Maybe I can. Maybe I can't. Either way is just fine." That makes a very big difference in the story! The American way is to set our jaw and push until we get through. The Asian way is to accept limits gracefully. Each view has its place. But in either case, the books we read make a big difference in the way we see the world. They can help us to find love, joy, and adventure.

The Adventure of Learning

Our first experiences with books may cause us to dread or to celebrate learning. Snuggling up for a nighttime tale changes how we see the world for a lifetime. Parents may share books with their children that help them discover love, joy, and adventure in their lives. And the snuggling that accompanies good parental storytelling has a message all its own.

We have always kept a good set of encyclopedias near our dining table. When our children or guests raise an interesting question, we grab the appropriate volume of the encyclopedia. For example, when one of our children said something about eating like a bird, we grabbed the B volume of the encyclopedia. On the way to *bird* we ran into *Bangladesh, barometer, bats, Betelgeuse, bile, Bolivia* (oops, overshot)—*bird!* Our encyclopedia has forty-seven pages about birds. We enjoyed photos showing the rich textures of their eggs, the colors of their plumage, and their wild diversity. Under "How Birds Get Food" we read that a tiny bird such as a kinglet is likely to eat as much as a third of its body weight every day!

Think about it! If I were a human kinglet, I could eat 57 pounds of enchiladas, tacos, boiled shrimp, and butter pecan ice cream every day! Eating like a bird takes on a whole new meaning!

Once a man from Delaware was visiting us. He commented that Delaware is a very small state. Small? How small? We turned to the encyclopedia. Well, Delaware has about two thousand square miles. We didn't have a very good idea of how big that is. So we looked up the area of Alabama, where we used to live: fifty-two thousand square miles. Alabama is twenty-six times as big as Delaware! Wow. But how does that compare with Texas? Texas, according to our encyclopedia, has almost 267,000 square miles. Texas is over 130 times as big as Delaware! How do their populations and population densities compare? How does this compare to Alaska? What are the principle economic bases for Delaware's economy? How vulnerable are they to economic reverses? The questions are limitless.

Isn't learning exciting! Fortunately we are not trying to trick our kids into a false belief. We merely need to follow our natural curiosity to the satisfying activity of learning.

There are many ways we show our love of learning. Do we have a valued book collection that has a central location in our home? Do we check out books from the library for recreational and educational purposes? Do we enjoy asking questions and looking for answers? Do we subscribe to magazines? Do we share our discoveries with one another? Do we make comfortable places for reading? In all that, do we provide for the different interests and styles of family members?

There are other ways to show our commitment to reading. One way is to provide a reading loft and bookshelf in a bedroom, such as in Andy's Western Town. Or to provide a comfortable reading room for the family. Another way is to disconnect the television from any antenna or cable. Sometimes we show our love of learning by choosing to discard less efficient activities (such as television watching) in favor of more efficient ones (such as conversation, outings, reading).

We can also make learning fun. Like a safari to the bookstore. A trip to a museum or historic site. Or by the way we read to each other.

Even though Sara is now sixteen, she has always loved to have me read her *The Maggie B* (Irene Haas [New York: Atheneum, 1984]), the story of a little girl who goes on a mythical night sea voyage with her baby brother James. As I read of the storm, I shout and howl. As we recount their quiet meal in the cabin, we snuggle warmly. We live the joyous journey of that creative girl and her beloved brother.

Jackie reads *Blueberries for Sal* by Robert McCloskey to her preschool class. As she reads of picking blueberries, she has one of her students drop blueberries into a bucket. Kuplink, kuplank, kuplunk! Children enjoy the mix-up with Sal and baby bear. And after reading the story, they love making the blueberries into jam to spread on fresh bread.

Books open an amazing world of love, joy, and adventure. Children's books have a unique way of delivering powerful messages clearly and beautifully. Consider a few classics.

Love

A great book about the cycle of life and love is *Miss Tizzy* by Libba Moore Gray. A characterful woman teaches the children to laugh and play and serve. When Miss Tizzy becomes ill, they know how to help.

Among the remarkable books about love is Hans de Beer's *Little Polar Bear Finds a Friend,* in which a little polar bear named Lars makes friends with animals taken captive for the zoo. Two particular friends include the walrus and Bea, a little brown bear. After a daring escape, the walrus guides the two bears to Lars's home in the frozen north. But as they head home, Lars worries about whether his parents will accept Bea, who is *brown*. When they arrive and Lars asks his dad if brown Bea can join them, Lars's father makes a classic statement: "That's silly. Bears are bears." The book ends with a southside illustration of Lars, his parents, and Bea heading north toward home. A beautiful statement about the oneness of all God's creatures!

Great children's books about love also show how human compassion can transcend political divisions. In *Rose Blanche* by Roberto Innocenti, a little girl in Nazi Germany is moved to reach out to captives who are hungry. *The Tunnel* by Anthony Browne shows how love outshines sibling rivalry. Eve Bunting's *The Wednesday Surprise* tells of a devoted girl who teaches her grandmother to read, which is a joyous surprise for the whole family. Two classics tell of connections across generations: *Watch the Stars Come Out* by Riki Levinson and *Now One Foot, Now the Other* by Tomie de Paola.

Appreciation of poor and homeless people is gently taught in DyAnne DiSalvo-Ryan's *Uncle Willie and the Soup Kitchen*. *Tacky the Penguin* by Helen Lester teaches us that being different can be good. In fact, Tacky can be as good as other characters: Goodly, Lovely, Angel, Neatly, and Perfect.

Children's books can also teach us about marriage. *Fanny's Dream* by Caralyn Buehner beautifully shows the love and adjustment that make marriage work. The rich illustrations enchant us. The story warms us.

Many of the great children's books operate at several levels. For example, *Santa Calls* by William Joyce appears at first to be a simple (and elegantly illustrated) adventure of a boy, his sister, and a friend to the North Pole. But the warm conclusion teaches us poignantly that the greatest gift of all is love.

Joy

Simple joy is one of the trademarks of great children's books. One of the classics is *The Jolly Postman* by Janet Ahlberg. In this beautifully illustrated story, an English postman delivers mail to familiar storybook characters. Accompanying the story are the actual little letters! So we get to read Goldilocks's apology to

Baby Bear. And the eviction notice to the wolf. And the postcard to the giant of beanstalk fame. Children of all ages delight in the story and in reading the clever letters. Appropriately, the story ends with Baby Bear joining Goldilocks at her birthday party.

June 29, 1999 by David Wiesner is a brilliant story of a little girl who sends up seeds with balloons only to find gigantic vegetables descending to earth. Imagine broccoli two stories tall! A delightful journey that stretches our imagination. And a surprise ending.

Some joys are gentle. *Home by Five* by Ruth Wallace-Brodeur takes us home from the skating rink with little Rosie as she rushes to get home on time. She passes up tempting side trips but still is late. A warm experience of childhood and an illustration of wise parents!

While many adult books are loud and demanding, great children's books are usually gentle. In *The Salamander Room* by Anne Mazer, a boy's room is transformed to accommodate his captured salamander. The result is a gentle and persuasive message that the right place for salamanders is where salamanders live. The book also invites us to connect with the beautiful natural world around us.

We learn joy in helping injured animals in *Nora's Duck* by Satomi Ichikawa. We laugh at our own misery in *Alexander and the Terrible, Horrible, No Good, Very Bad Day* by Judith Viorst. In *Amazing Grace* by Mary Hoffman, we experience the triumph of a determined black girl named Grace who wants to play Peter Pan. In all of these books there are joyous endings, whether exuberant or serene.

Adventure

For the child with a spirit of adventure, there are great books that can act as inspired guides. Chris Van Allsburg has changed the way we see our world. In *Jumanji* he brings a jungle adventure right into our home! In *The Mysteries of Harris Burdick* he invites us to write our own adventure stories around his haunting illustrations.

Arthur Getz's *Tar Beach* shows us that when money is scarce, adventure may take us to our own rooftop. *The Trouble with*

Grandad (New York: G. P. Putnam's Sons, 1988) takes us on one of Babette Cole's irrepressible journeys. One of the delights of *Escape of Marvin the Ape* by Caralyn Buehner is the premise that an escaped ape could pass himself off as a native New Yorker. Classic story with rich illustrations!

Millicent and the Wind by Robert N. Munsch teaches us of friendship. *Five Minutes' Peace* by Jill Murphy shows the challenge of motherhood. George Ella Lyon's *Come a Tide* carries us through a flood with grit and humor.

If you want to teach your children to use ingenuity and to respect themselves, *Paper Bag Princess* by Robert N. Munsch is a perfect book. When a princess is scorched by a dragon who steals the prince, she dons a paper bag and conjures a wise strategy. She conquers the dragon and saves the prince. And, in the end, she shows that the best way to be happy may be different from many storybook endings.

In addition to children's storybooks are a wide range of visual dictionaries, field guides, and encyclopedias that teach and amaze. What once may have been inaccessible to children is now delightful and understandable.

Children's books are good for children. But, wisely chosen, they challenge and delight adults as well. A wise parent lets his or her delight show in the book. The wise parent makes reading time a special time. The wise parent asks thought-provoking questions. The wise parent makes learning fun.

Our living legacy to future generations is our children. We can make our message loving, joyous, and adventurous as we fill our children with warmth and wisdom, hope and joy.

Recommended children's books about love that are described in the text:

Anthony Browne, *The Tunnel* (New York: Knopf, 1989).
Caralyn Buehner, *Fanny's Dream* (New York: Dial Books, 1995).
Eve Bunting, *The Wednesday Surprise* (New York: Clarion Books, 1989).
Hans de Beer, *Little Polar Bear Finds a Friend* (New York: North-South Books, 1990).

Tomie de Paola, *Now One Foot, Now the Other* (New York: Putnam, 1981).

DyAnne DiSalvo-Ryan, *Uncle Willie and the Soup Kitchen* (New York: Morrow Junior Books, 1991).

Libba Moore Gray, *Miss Tizzy* (New York: Simon & Schuster, 1993).

Irene Haas, *The Maggie B.* (New York: Atheneum, 1984).

Roberto Innocenti, *Rose Blanche* (Mankonto, Minnesota: Creative Education, 1985).

William Joyce, *Santa Calls* (New York: HarperCollins, 1993).

Helen Lester, *Tacky the Penguin* (Boston: Houghton Mifflin Co., 1988).

Riki Levinson, *Watch the Stars Come Out* (New York: Dutton, 1985).

Robert McCloskey, *Blueberries for Sal* (New York: Viking Press, 1948).

Additional great children's books about love:

Lena Anderson, *Bunny Party* (New York: R & S Books, 1987).

Natalie Babbitt, *Bub or The Very Best Thing* (New York: HarperCollins, 1994).

Nick Butterworth, *My Dad Is Awesome* (Cambridge, Massachusetts: Candlewick Press, 1989).

Kevin Henkes, *Chrysanthemum* (New York: Greenwillow Books, 1991).

George Ella Lyon, *Cecil's Story* (New York: Orchard Books, 1991).

Sam McBratney, *Guess How Much I Love You* (Cambridge, Massachusetts: Candlewick Press, 1995).

Junko Morimoto, *My Hiroshima* (New York: Viking, 1990).

Robert N. Munsch, *Love You Forever* (Scarborough, Ontario: Firefly Books, 1986).

John Steptoe, *Mufaro's Beautiful Daughters: An African Tale* (New York: Lothrop, Lee & Shepard Books, 1987).

Ann Warren Turner, *Nettie's Trip South* (New York: Macmillan, 1987).

Ann Warren Turner, *Through Moon and Stars and Night Skies* (New York: Harper and Row, 1990).

Mary K. Whittington, *The Patchwork Lady* (San Diego: Harcourt-Brace Jovanovich, 1991).

Vera B. Williams, *A Chair for My Mother* (New York: Greenwillow Books, 1982).

Recommended children's books about joy that are described in the text:

Janet and Allan Ahlberg, *The Jolly Postman or Other People's Letters* (Boston: Little, Brown, 1986).

Mary Hoffman, *Amazing Grace* (New York: Dial Books, 1991).

Satomi Ichikawa, *Nora's Duck* (New York: Philomel Books, 1991).

Ann Mazer, *The Salamander Room* (New York: Knopf, 1991).

Judith Viorst, *Alexander and the Terrible, Horrible, No Good, Very Bad Day* (New York: Atheneum, 1972).

Ruth Wallace-Brodeur, *Home by Five* (New York: M. K. McElderry Books, 1992).

David Wiesner, *June 29, 1999* (New York: Clarion Books, 1992).

Additional great children's books about joy:

Janet and Allan Ahlberg, *Peek-A-Boo!* (New York: Viking Press, 1981).

Camilla Ashforth, *Horatio's Bed* (Cambridge, Massachusetts: Candlewick Press, 1992).

Mary Barwick, *The Alabama Angels* (Montgomery, Alabama: Black Belt Press, 1990).

Nick Butterworth, *The Nativity Play* (Boston: Little, Brown, 1985).

Joanna Cole, *Who Put the Pepper in the Pot?* (New York: Parents Magazine Press, 1989).

Christophe Gallaz, *Threadbear* (Mankato, Minnesota: Creative Education, 1993).

Satomi Ichikawa, *Bravo, Tanya* (New York: Philomel Books, 1992).

Satomi Ichikawa, *Nora's Roses* (New York: Philomel Books, 1993).

Satomi Ichikawa, *Nora's Stars* (New York: Philomel Books, 1988).

Riki Levinson, *Our Home is the Sea* (New York: E. P. Dutton, 1988).

Kim Lewis, *First Snow* (Cambridge, Massachusetts: Candlewick Press, 1993).

Robert McCloskey, *One Morning in Maine* (New York: Viking Press, 1952).

Robert N. Munsch, *Murmel, Murmel, Murmel* (Scarborough, Ontario: Annick Press, 1982).

Helen Oxenbury, *Tom and Pippo Read a Story* (New York: Aladdin Books, 1988).

Peter Spier, *Bored—Nothing to Do!* (Garden City, New York: Doubleday, 1978).

Martin Waddell, *Can't You Sleep, Little Bear?* (Cambridge, Massachusetts: Candlewick Press, 1988).

Recommended children's books about adventure that are described in the text:

Caralyn Buehner, *The Escape of Marvin the Ape* (New York: Dial Books, 1992).

Babette Cole, *The Trouble with Grandad* (New York: G. P. Putnam's Sons, 1988).

George Ella Lyon, *Come a Tide* (New York: Orchard Books, 1990).

Robert N. Munsch, *Millicent and the Wind* (Scarborough, Ontario: Annick Press, 1984).

Robert N. Munsch, *Paper Bag Princess* (Scarborough, Ontario: Annick Press, 1980).

Jill Murphy, *Five Minutes' Peace* (New York: Putnam, 1986).

Faith Ringgold, *Tar Beach* (New York: Crown Publishers, 1991).

Chris Van Allsburg, *Jumanji* (Boston: Houghton Mifflin Co., 1981).

Chris Van Allsburg, *The Mysteries of Harris Burdick* (Boston: Houghton Mifflin Co., 1984).

Additional great children's books about adventure:

Jez Alborough, *Where's My Teddy?* (Cambridge, Massachusetts: Candlewick, 1992).

Christine Berry, *Mama Went Walking* (New York: Henry Holt, 1990).

Hans de Beer, *Ahoy There, Little Polar Bear* (New York: North-South Books, 1995).

Hans de Beer, *Little Polar Bear* (New York: North-South Books, 1987).

Monique Felix, *The Story of a Little Mouse Trapped in a Book* (La Jolla, California: Green Tiger Press, 1980).

Anna Fienberg, *The Hottest Boy Who Ever Lived* (Morton Grove, Illinois: Albert Whitman, 1993).

Patricia Lee Gauch, *Christina Katerina and the Great Bear Train* (New York: Putnam, 1990).

Diane Goode, *I Hear a Noise* (New York: Dutton, 1988).

James Gurney, *James Gurney's Dinotopia* (Atlanta: Turner Publishing, 1993).

Barbara Shook Hazen, *The Knight Who Was Afraid of the Dark* (New York: Dial Books, 1989).

Emily Arnold McCully, *Mirette on the High Wire* (New York: G. P. Putnam's Sons, 1992).

Peggy Rathmann, *Good Night, Gorilla* (New York: Putnam, 1994).

Diane Stanley, *Moe the Dog in Tropical Paradise* (New York: Putnam, 1992).

Colin Thompson, *Looking for Atlantis* (New York: Knopf, 1994).

Eugene Trivizas, *Three Little Wolves and the Big Bad Pig* (New York: Maxwell Macmillan International, 1993).

Chris Van Allsburg, *The Sweetest Fig* (Boston: Houghton Mifflin Co., 1993).

Chris Van Allsburg, *The Widow's Broom* (Boston: Houghton Mifflin Co., 1992).

Martin Waddell, *The Pig in the Pond* (Cambridge, Massachusetts: Candlewick Press, 1992).

David Wiesner, *Tuesday* (New York: Clarion Books, 1991).

Steve Wunderli, *Marty's World* (Salt Lake City: Bookcraft, 1986).

Some great children's nonfiction:

Carol Anne Campbell, *Wildflower Field Guide* (New York: Workman, 1993).

Ted Dewan, *Inside the Whale and Other Animals* (New York: Doubleday, 1992).

Eyewitness Visual Dictionaries (New York: Dorling Kindersley).

Maryjo Koch, *Bird, Egg, Feather, Nest* (New York: Stewart, Tabori, & Chang, 1992).

Patrick Moore, *Astronomy for the Beginner* (New York: Cambridge University Press, 1992).

Philip and Phylis Morrison, *Powers of Ten: A Book about the Relative Size of Things in the Universe* (Redding, Connecticut: Scientific American Library, 1982).

See and Explore Library (New York: Dorling Kindersley).

Joseph E. Wallace, *Familiar Dinosaurs* (New York: Knopf, 1993).

Twenty-Two

TEACHING CHILDREN TO BELIEVE

Therefore shall ye lay up these my words in your heart and in your soul, and bind them for a sign upon your hand. . . . And ye shall teach them your children.
—Deuteronomy 11:18–19

It can be a great surprise to find out what our children rank as the great miracles of their lives. When I asked our Andy about the greatest miracle of his life, he reminded me of the summer we chose our family vacation specifically to look at places where we were interested in moving. The trip took us a thousand miles from home. As we were traveling along toward our appointed goal, Nancy suggested that we stop and see some old friends in an obscure town along the way. I resisted, not wanting to waste vacation time. But Nancy prevailed. When we stopped for lunch, Nancy called ahead to arrange the visit. We were surprised to find that the family was moving on that very day. We were dismayed to find that the husband and wife were moving to different cities, ending years of marriage and dividing their beautiful young family. We arranged to visit anyway. When we arrived at their home, we helped the wife and her visiting parents load their trailer. Then Nancy, troubled by the dissolution of this covenant relationship, took me aside and suggested that I visit the husband, who was still at work. Again I resisted. I supposed that I should have some kind of counsel, help, or encouragement to offer the husband. But I had no idea what to say. It seemed best to avoid the whole embarrassing situation. But again Nancy prevailed.

I visited the man working late at the office. We exchanged pleasantries. Then I dove in. I asked how we could help. He asked a few tentative questions. I gave the best counsel I knew to give. We may have talked for an hour. Then we parted. I picked up my family, and we continued on our vacation.

Later that man wrote and said that when I walked through the door, he knew he was in trouble. I had served years earlier as his bishop. It seemed marvelous that on the very day that his marriage partnership was ending, we would appear at his office more than a thousand miles from our home and totally ignorant of their situation. It is now some years since that chance visit. The husband and wife reunited shortly after our visit. Their challenges have not disappeared. But they are continuing to work at building an eternal relationship.

I know that we did not do anything that fixed their marriage. But I also know that Heavenly Father can send his messages via his imperfect children. Our very appearance sent a powerful message to that family. It reminded them of an earlier, better time. It reminded them that we all struggle and make mistakes but keep trying. Somehow Heavenly Father orchestrated many events to send a powerful message to two of his struggling children.

That is a miracle. When we left that couple, we said very little about the experience. But we acknowledged that it was amazing, and we prayed that Heavenly Father would bless that family. An incident that we hardly expected our children to remember was still blessing their lives years later. For Andy, it still felt joyous to have been a part of one of the Father's miracles. "Search diligently, pray always, and be believing, and all things shall work together for your good, if ye walk uprightly and remember the covenant wherewith ye have covenanted one with another" (D&C 90:24). The whole family may be blessed by inviting our children to share with us the miracles they see in their lives. Also, we may be surprised how our families are blessed when we share our own experience of seeing God acting to bless and teach us.

The most important lessons of believing may be taught at home. Faith is a way of seeing the world. It is acknowledging that Heavenly Father is able to do his work. It is recognizing that things can make sense even when we do not understand them. That is a vital lesson for all of us. It is an important lesson for children to learn while yet young.

Nancy had a miscarriage some time after Andy was born. We were sad. But in time Nancy became pregnant again, and our hopes were renewed. The pregnancy progressed well, until one day Nancy began to bleed. We rushed her to the doctor. He did what he could but made no promises. We gave Nancy a priesthood blessing. We prayed. But Nancy continued to move toward another miscarriage. I went alone into our backyard, where I prayed: "Father, we are trying to do what is right. We are not asking for anything bad. Please bless Nancy so that she will not miscarry." Begging progressed into demanding. And even threatening.

But Nancy miscarried nonetheless. I wondered what good could come of that. I was hurt and angry. Now, years later and about twenty miscarriages later, I can name many blessings that came from our painful experience. We cherish every child, especially Sara, who came in the midst of the miscarriages. We have learned to trust Heavenly Father to make a blessing of every experience. We have learned to say, "We are all right." We have learned to be patient in understanding his will. Our children have been a part of the continuing struggle to trust with all our hearts. They are learning faith along with us.

Great-Grandma Wright had eleven children who kept her very busy. She struggled to provide for them with the family's limited resources. Life was hard. She looked forward to that time in her life when the children would be grown and she would have time for her neglected hobbies: reading and sewing. After many years the children grew up and left home. Grandma had time. And she went blind. My father remembers visiting his grandma and asking, "Grandma, how are you?" Her standard response was, "I'm all right. I'm all right." (I love to hear my dear father say those serene words!) Blessed by the comforts of faith, Grandma learned to sew coarse fabric with darning needles. Family members could read to her. She was all right. Her example of faith has warmed and blessed my life and my children's lives.

One of the ironies of mortality is that life often takes what seems most dear so that we may come to know what matters even more. So those words, "I'm all right," have become code words in our family. They mean that we trust the Father. We believe that he knows better than we do how to teach and bless us. We believe that he has not lost control of the universe. Nor has he lost track of our struggles and needs. "Are not two sparrows sold for a farthing? and one of them shall not fall on the ground without your Father. But the very hairs of your head are all numbered. Fear ye not therefore, ye are of more value than many sparrows." (Matthew 10:29–31.)

Faith is not merely something we teach. It is something we live. If we are nurturing an active, vital faith, it will show in a thousand ways, many that we would not have guessed. Wise parents will join with their children in staying alert for the hand of God.

Glenn Tinder pointed out a common unenlightened attitude: "Perhaps discussions of religion would be more fruitful if we could rid ourselves of the assumption, common among Christians and practically universal among non-Christians, that God is simple-minded. We readily grant that a great writer such as Joyce or Proust is infinitely subtle and resourceful in fashioning a novel; but we assume that in fashioning human history God will be heavy-handed and obvious. Accordingly, some believers conclude that they know exactly what God has in mind and, vested with high office, could provide him with some much needed help. . . . Unbelievers conclude that they know what God would do if he existed, and that since those things are not being done, he does not exist." ("Glenn Tinder Replies," *Atlantic* 265:12.)

Elder Neal A. Maxwell has recommended that our trust of Heavenly Father go beyond trusting his grand design: "Becoming a true believer . . . means trusting not only in the Lord's plan for all of mankind but especially trusting in His unfolding and particularized plan for each of us" ("True Believers in Christ," in *1980 Devotional Speeches of the Year* [Provo, Utah: Brigham Young University Press, 1981], p. 136).

Parents can inspire their children by bringing stories of scriptural heroes to life with personal understanding. For example, we can teach our children about Moses as a hero of faith when he stood on the edge of the Red Sea hemmed in by unbelieving children of Israel and the attacking armies of Pharaoh. Was he serene? Did he struggle? I suspect that he struggled much as we do in our lives as we try to determine what Heavenly Father would have us do. What we know for sure is that Moses used the power of God to lead the people to safety. Moses is a hero. We can bless our children with his example as we teach them not only of his triumphs but of his struggles. He resisted God's call because he did not think he could lead the children of Israel. He wrestled with the restlessness and unbelief of the people and the hard-heartedness of Pharaoh. Moses struggled. So do we. Home evenings and family scripture study can be places where we come to know, admire, and take practical lessons from scriptural heroes and even those in our own families and neighborhoods.

In that interval between a painful event and the vision of its purpose, we may choose to believe even though we do not fully understand. The interval may be a lifetime. But listening to whisperings that hint at eternal meanings, we may trust. "And we talk of Christ, we rejoice in Christ, we preach of Christ, we prophesy of Christ, and we write according to our prophecies, that our children may know to what source they may look for a remission of their sins" (2 Nephi 25:26). There are many ways that we teach our children to have faith. The obvious ones are familiar: family home evening, church attendance, scripture study, and prayer. Even in those practices, the difference between a vibrant energy and a dead form are clear. For instance, in home evening we can dread and resent the wasted time or we can find high drama and personal insight in Enoch's vision, Elijah's journey, Nephi's psalm, and King Benjamin's counsel. But only if we have brought our hearts to the study.

There are many great ideas and books about faith. When we share our life experiences and the best thinking of other earnest believers, we can help our family members nurture faith. (Some quotes about believing are provided at the end of this chapter.)

There are other ways that our commitments are evident. When my young siblings and I grew restless on long car trips, mother led us in Primary songs. Mom taught us joy in music. She also taught us that believing can fill the empty places.

Now we feel blessed by our children's growing expressions of faith. Emily wrote from her mission in Belgium: "I didn't feel familiar with the discussion and that made me depend more on the Lord—and it was great! We need strategy, but we need to let the Captain lead the army!"

The single most powerful way we can teach our children may be in those troubled times when we honestly but hopefully wrestle to find meaning and finally allow that God may have a purpose beyond our understanding. Heavenly Father can bless us in many ways. He may not bless us in the ways that make sense to us. But he is committed to helping us grow. And bless us he will.

Some Quotes about Believing

There are many great ideas and books about faith. With your family you might share your favorite scriptures, quotes, and life experiences. In addition, the following excerpts from H. E. Fosdick's book titled *The Meaning of Faith* (New York: Association Press, 1918) might be of interest to older children and adults who are interested in understanding faith.

"We must believe that there is a purpose running through the stern, forbidding process. What men have needed most of all in suffering, is not to know the explanation, but to know that there is an explanation. And religious faith alone gives confidence that human tragedy is not the meaningless sport of physical forces, making our life what Voltaire called it, 'a bad joke.'" (*Meaning of Faith*, p. 20.)

"Bernard Shaw: 'What a man believes may be ascertained not from his creed, but from the assumptions on which he habitually acts.' . . . He tends to face suffering either hopefully as a school of moral discipline, in a world presided over by a Father, or grimly as a hardship in which there is no meaning." (*Meaning of Faith*, p. 24.)

" 'Oh God, too near to be found, too simple to be conceived, too good to be believed. . . . Show us how foolish it is to doubt Thee, since Thou Thyself dost set questions which disturb us; reveal our unbelief to be faith fretting at its out worn form. . . . Teach us to trust not to cleverness or learning, but to that inward faith which can never be denied. Lead us out of confusion to simplicity. Call us back from wandering without to find Thee at home within.' W. E. Orchard." (*Meaning of Faith*, p. 34.)

"Doubt, therefore, does have real value in life; it clears away rubbish and stimulates search for truth; but it has no value unless it is finally swallowed up in positive assurance" (*Meaning of Faith*, p. 30).

"George Macdonald: 'Each generation must do its own seeking and finding. The father's having found is only the warrant for the children's search.'" (*Meaning of Faith*, p. 43.)

"Every exaltation, every pure sentiment, all urgency of true affection, and all yearning after things higher and nobler, are testimonies of the divinity that is in us" (*Meaning of Faith*, p. 89).

"The insolvency of 'belief' was due to the bankruptcy of 'trust.' . . . The peril of religion is that vital experience shall be resolved into a formula of explanation, and that men, grasping the formula, shall suppose themselves thereby to possess the experience." (*Meaning of Faith*, p. 101.)

"How can I believe that my existence and my purpose are not a cruel joke unless I am begotten by a Spiritual Life that will sustain my strength and crown my effort? To believe that man's soul is a foundling, laid on the doorstep of a merely physical universe, crying in vain for any father who begot him or any mother who conceived him, is to make our highest life a liar." (*Meaning of Faith*, p. 110.)

"No argument for the Christian experience can be quite so convincing as the Christian experience itself" (*Meaning of Faith*, p. 117).

"How seldom one finds enthusiastic unbelievers!" (*Meaning of Faith*, p. 124.)

"Stevenson has expressed their faith: 'If I from my spy-hole, looking with purblind [partially blind] eyes upon a least part of a fraction of the universe, yet perceive in my own destiny some broken evidences of a plan, and some signals of an overruling goodness; shall I then be so mad as to complain that all cannot be deciphered? Shall I not rather wonder, with infinite and grateful surprise, that in so vast a scheme I seem to have been able to read, however little, and that little was encouraging to faith?'" (*Meaning of Faith*, pp. 138–39.)

"If we deny God, then goodness is a mystery" (*Meaning of Faith*, p. 148).

"Even where we fall feebly short of the ideal, we have no question what the ideal is. When in biography or among our friends we see folk face crushing trouble, not embittered by it, made cynical, or thrust into despair, but hallowed, sweetened, illumined, and empowered, we are aware that noble characters do not *bear* trouble; they *use* it." (*Meaning of Faith*, p. 149; emphasis in original.)

"It becomes more clear the more one ponders it, that while this is often a hard world in which to be happy, to men of insight and faith it may be a great world in which to build character" (*Meaning of Faith*, p. 151).

" 'The trouble seems to be that God is not in a hurry and I am.' Theodore Parker." (*Meaning of Faith*, p. 154; see also p. 156.)

"Folks work joyfully at a picture-puzzle so long as they believe that the puzzle can be put together. . . . But if they begin to fear that they are being fooled, that the puzzle is a hoax and never can be pieced together anywhere by anyone, how swiftly that suspicion will benumb their work." (*Meaning of Faith*, pp. 194–95.)

"Are we to trust for our guidance the testimony of our worse or better hours? . . . We have cellars in our houses. But we do not live there; we live upstairs!" (*Meaning of Faith*, p. 203.)

"What do we value most when we rise toward our best?" (*Meaning of Faith*, p. 207.)

"The very fact that we are here means that he does believe in us, in our possibilities of growth, in our capacities of service, in what he can do in and for and through us before he is done" (*Meaning of Faith*, p. 212).

"Fill us with Thyself, that we may no longer be a burden to ourselves" (*Meaning of Faith*, p. 213).

"Salamander's eggs act as though they were seriously intent on making salamanders. Purpose is essential in the description of every living thing." (*Meaning of Faith*, p. 223.)

Twenty-Three

TEACHING REPENTANCE
AND RENEWAL

The Spirit of the Lord Omnipotent . . .
has wrought a mighty change in us, or in our hearts,
that we have no more disposition to do evil,
but to do good continually.
—Mosiah 5:2

Repentance has gloomy overtones. It suggests embarrassment, suffering, estrangement. Any who have felt the need to confess error to an ecclesiastical leader may have had any of several reactions: "Why should I tell him? It's none of his business!" "It won't do any good to confess. I make the same mistakes over and over and over. It just doesn't matter. I can't change." "It's no big deal. Everyone makes mistakes. If I just live right, maybe I can put it behind me."

Understanding true processes of repentance is vitally important for people who will attempt to teach children the principles of eternal progress. How we respond to our own mistakes and to their mistakes teaches them a pattern. That pattern can cause them to feel overwhelmed, hopeless, hostile, indifferent, and worthless. Or it can cause them to feel penitent, hopeful, and a yearning to be clean. Repentance leads to joy. "Create in me a clean heart, O God; and renew a right spirit within me" (Psalm 51:10).

Much of the bad press for repentance relates to the inversion described in chapter one. Satan would have us believe that he and his followers are the ones who have all the fun while the Father and his friends suffer patiently, knowing that they are doing what is right even if they never have fun. Of course, such ideas are a total inversion.

Wickedness never was happiness! (See Alma 41:10.) Following Satan leads to ever-greater cravings and ever-smaller enjoyments.

Drugs are an example of how Satan works. They offer an explosion of pleasure. They promise freedom and vision. But even as they arouse us, they deaden us. They permanently damage our ability to take any pleasure in anything. More and more chemical is required to feel any pleasure. They enslave us as they destroy us. Satan is the father of lies.

That is different from God, who is the gracious Giver of life. With remarkable efficiency, whenever his Spirit is with us he comforts, teaches, and cleanses all at once. Whenever he has visited, we are better for it. Freer. Happier. Finer. The commandments are the directions of an all-wise Father for discovering happiness.

Jeffrey R. Holland has given us a fresh perspective on repentance. "Repentance is simply the scriptural invitation for growth and improvement and progress and renewal. You can change! You can be anything you want to be in righteousness." ("For Times of Trouble," in *1980 Devotional Speeches of the Year* [Provo, Utah: Brigham Young University Press, 1981], p. 42.)

Consider how that definition fits with scriptural instances of repentance. Alma is the classic case. Though of chosen lineage, he went about destroying the children of God. Because of his extreme destructiveness and the faith of his father, his reckless behavior was interrupted by an angel. When confronted with his sins by the angel, Alma "was racked with eternal torment" (Alma 36:12), "tormented with the pains of hell" (Alma 36:13), and racked "with inexpressible horror" (Alma 36:14) and "the pains of a damned soul" (Alma 36:16). Those are the fruits of being in Satan's employ.

How did Alma react to his inexpressible misery? "I remembered also to have heard my father prophesy unto the people concerning the coming of one Jesus Christ, a Son of God, to atone for the sins of the world. Now, as my mind caught hold upon this thought, I cried within my heart: O Jesus, thou Son of God, have mercy on me, who am in the gall of bitterness, and am encircled about by the everlasting chains of death." (Alma 36:17–18.)

Apparently Alma felt that he was about to be destroyed. In his abject misery he recognized that his only hope, a seemingly desperate hope, was to call upon that Jesus of whom he had heard his father speak. What was the result of his urgent plea? Did God respond in this spirit: "Alma, you have been a despicable and troublesome little fellow. You need to show your sincerity by suffering for a decade or two. You need to learn a lesson. Then I may bless you"? No. Despite Alma's being undeserving, the Father responded in a way we could hardly expect: "When I thought this, I could remember my pains no more. . . . And oh, what joy, and what marvelous light I did behold; yea, my soul was filled with joy as exceeding as was my pain! . . . [T]here can be nothing so exquisite and sweet as was my joy." (Alma 36: 19–21.)

That is remarkable! By calling upon the Savior and subjecting himself to his will, Alma was transformed! He still spent a lifetime in service. His repentance was not complete until he had endured to the end. But the Book of Mormon's unmistakable message in Alma's powerful account appears to be that all salvation hinges on one thing: submitting to the redemption that is in Christ Jesus.

Jesus' words to the woman taken in adultery seem to have the same message as Alma's experience. "He said unto her, Woman, where are those thine accusers? hath no man condemned thee? She said, No man, Lord. And Jesus said unto her, Neither do I condemn thee: go, and sin no more." (John 8:10–11.) While the woman would spend the balance of her life establishing her cleanliness, the Lord offered immediate warmth, acceptance, encouragement, and love. How different from the common human reaction to error! We generally want people (including ourselves) to suffer for errors. Jesus wants us to be wiser and better. He can make us clean.

Several points about Heavenly Father's plan are clear. The first point is our abysmal unworthiness. King Benjamin stresses it: "And they had viewed themselves in their own carnal state, even less than the dust of the earth" (Mosiah 4:2). Moses was shocked by it: "Now, for this cause I know that man is nothing, which thing I never had supposed" (Moses 1:10). Jesus taught it dramatically in his parable of the unforgiving servant who, having been forgiven his large debt, was unwilling to forgive a small debt (see Matthew 18:23–35). In our fallen state, we are simply undeserving of his immeasurable goodness.

The second point is that the Lord wants to rescue and redeem us. He paid an infinite and eternal price. No debt we have ever incurred can strain his resources. So he reaches out to those who are, in our eyes, corrupt but to His eyes are earnest, seeking, and noble. "Is my hand shortened at all, that it cannot redeem?" (Isaiah 50:2.)

Jesus scandalized his Jewish contemporaries by forgiving grievous sinners. Time and again he offered not only fellowship but forgiveness to adulterers and sinners (see Matthew 9:1–8; Luke 7:36–50; John 4:7–30; John 8:1–11). His story of the prodigal is remarkably powerful as a great Christian message. Though the prodigal had behaved foolishly, sinfully, and wastefully, he was welcomed home with the robe, the ring, and the fatted calf when he had done nothing more than become hungry and miserable enough to turn toward home. He had been humbled, and he hungered for something better. Elder Neal A. Maxwell said, the true believer's "generosity reassures the repentant and also beckons the almost-repentant who warily probe the possibility of both fellowship and forgiveness" ("True Believers in Christ," in *1980 Devotional Speeches of the Year* [Provo, Utah: Brigham Young University Press, 1981], p. 138).

What are the lessons of repentance that we can learn from the Savior and apply in our homes?

1. Heavenly Father gives us a myriad of teachers and reminders of eternal law. He teaches us the true path to joy. The landscape is dotted with redemptive reminders. He invites and entices to his joyous lifestyle. He unfailingly makes his invitation of joy and redemption. We may do the same with our children. Children must be accountable for their acts, but we may provide a system that makes success likely. We offer choices that are appropriate for their maturity. We teach them principles of choice and accountability. We help them see their choices and the results associated with them. We show them that they can learn from their mistakes and become better.

2. Heavenly Father values free agency so much that he allows us to make bad decisions. He does not force, compel, demand,

or insist. But he does allow us to discover the pain associated with sin. We are allowed to glimpse the pain of hell so that we may know that it is not what we want. We learn that there are consequences associated with choices. Likewise, wise parents allow their children to experience the natural consequences of their choices, but they are never glad to have their children suffer.

3. Everyone makes mistakes. Lots of mistakes. We can learn to make fewer mistakes. And we can learn from our mistakes. But we will make mistakes. We should respond to our children's mistakes by asking, "What did you learn from your experience?" rather than with an accusation such as, "What is wrong with you?" We should turn them toward the power that can cleanse and redeem. The Savior provided a revolutionary definition of righteousness when he defined the self-righteous Pharisee as a sinner and the penitent but sinful publican as a worthy model (see Luke 18:10–14).

4. There is only one way to be redeemed: through the Lord Jesus Christ. Only in and through him is salvation operative. He has paid the infinite and eternal price so that we may be redeemed if we will. Having applied his sacrifice in our lives, we should sing the song of redeeming love to our children, inviting them to apply his atonement in their lives.

5. Heavenly Father's objective is to teach us rather than to punish us. Bertrand Russell was probably right: "The reformative effect of punishment is a belief that dies hard, chiefly, I think, because it [punishment] is so satisfying to our sadistic impulses" (in Laurence J. Peter, comp., *Peter's Quotations* [New York: William Morrow and Co., 1977], p. 126; brackets in source). Humans tend to think that our suffering is the key to forgiveness. The Lord teaches that submitting to him and accepting his suffering is the key to forgiveness. When as parents we feel a strong urge to punish, it is not from the Father. If we follow his example we will teach our children with gentleness, meekness, and love unfeigned (see D&C 121:41).

Children's bad choices may, at times, result in the suspension of certain blessings. That suspension is different from punishment. It helps them learn the lofty value of blessings often taken for granted. The suspension should be clearly related to the offense.

6. Being earnest is not enough. The Lord expects us to be wise. We should teach our children practical skills for dealing with temptation and sin. For example, we can teach our children to make their decisions ahead of time; to use distractions such as singing hymns or getting busy when Satan is demanding our attention; to have social skills for getting out of difficult situations, such as saying, "I couldn't do that! My dad would kill me!"; and to recognize the discomfort of trying to justify bad choices.

7. The measure of true repentance is not the absence of sins but the theme of service and devotion that fills the reformed life. Just as King Benjamin suggested, no sooner have you attempted to pay God than he blesses you and puts you ever more in his debt. Repentant persons are not perfect, but they are earnest. Our children's desire to learn and do better should be cherished and encouraged. We can be gracious in offering love and mercy to those we serve, just as he has done with us.

8. The knowledge that matters is the knowledge of the Lord. Adam and Eve were tempted to partake of the fruit of the tree of knowledge of good and evil. Today we are still tempted to be curious about things we do not need to know. Sickness and perversion do not have to be studied. It is okay to be naive in worldly things while being wise in the things of God.

Parenting often progresses in stages. When our children are small and we are relatively inexperienced, we tend to be preoccupied with control and behavior management. As we and they get older, we change our focus. We become less interested in managing their behavior and more interested in having a relationship with them. Notice the way grandparents treat their grandchildren. Many of them have learned that a relationship is better than management. Children need to know that they can make mistakes and adults will still value them and want to have a continuing relationship with them.

As a child, Emily had trouble with coming home on time. So when we had planned an important family visit to a dear and troubled friend, we made sure that Emily, then about thirteen years of age, had the appointment and its importance clearly in mind. Still, when the appointed time came she was not to be found. She was last seen visiting with the neighbor girl. But we could not locate her anywhere now. We were frustrated. Our emotion was intensified by the fact that she had taken Sara with her and both of them would miss the important meeting as a result of her carelessness. Finally we went to the meeting without her. After the meeting, on our way home Nancy and I consulted about Emily's transgression. We were sure that she had understood the expectation. So we talked about various strong punishments. When we arrived home, we found Emily sitting sheepishly in the living room. I had mentally prepared my vitriolic sermon about responsibility, consideration, and consequences. As a perfunctory preliminary I asked her what excuse she had for missing our meeting. She said, "Dad, I'm sorry. After I visited with Betsy, I thought I would take a few minutes to visit with Millie down the street." Millie was a beloved eighty-year-old widow. "I was sure I could get back in time, but Millie started telling me stories and I didn't know how to get away. I'm sorry." It would have been easier to be mad at Emily, except I had been caught by Millie before and had found myself, even at almost forty years old, unable to get away. We talked with Emily about planning ahead and letting us know where she was. But we also expressed our joy that she would initiate a visit to a widow out of the goodness of her heart.

When as parents we take the role of judge, we usually fail to appreciate the earnestness of our children. We are more likely to notice the inconvenience that results from their irresponsibility. The irony should be obvious. Consider how eternally inconvenient we are for our Heavenly Father. Yet he, loving us as he does, continues to bless and teach us. How many times he has in essence said, "Despite your remarkable sins, my hand is stretched out still!" (Such an invitation is pronounced five times in Isaiah and repeated five times by Nephi! For example: "For all this his anger is not turned away, but his hand is stretched out still" (2 Nephi 15:25). He wants to redeem us from our sins!

When we as parents are humbly mindful of his graciousness with us, we are more likely to be appropriately gracious with our children. He recommends that, even after we have provided our children needed correction, we show "forth afterwards an increase of love toward him whom thou hast reproved, lest he esteem thee to be his enemy; that he may know that thy faithfulness is stronger than the cords of death" (D&C 121:43–44).

Faithfulness stronger than the cords of death! That is faithfulness! Heavenly graciousness does not mean that we ignore children's offenses. It does mean that we help children make amends, learn the lessons, and feel hopeful. It also means that we make allowances for the unique way that each child learns.

Cesare Beccaria said: "The fault no child ever loses is the one he was most punished for" (in *Peter's Quotations*, p. 82). Sometimes we label our children with certain faults in ways that make it more likely that they will not only continue in that fault but identify themselves as that kind of person. But we can help our children "get deservingly reclassified" (Neal A. Maxwell, "True Believers in Christ," in *1980 Devotional Speeches of the Year*, p. 138) by inviting them to learn, change, and grow.

Note the powerful teaching tool the Savior uses with us. Every week he invites us to come to the sacrament table, where he offers the emblems of his sacrifice so that we might be healed, cleansed, and renewed. If we really believe that the sacrament is a renewal of baptism, then every week we may start again clean and refreshed. He invites us to "come boldly unto the throne of grace" (Hebrews 4:16). Oh, that we might be as gracious with our children! How hopeful they would feel if we responded to their mistakes in the same redemptive spirit that he responds to ours!

Twenty-Four

USING THE PRINCIPLE
OF PRAYER

And they shall also teach their children to pray.
—D&C 68:28

"Do you believe in personal revelation?" someone asked.

"Yes and no," was my instinctive reply. "If by personal revelation you mean that God will tell us everything to do if we just listen to him, my answer is no. If by personal revelation you mean that the Father will advise, teach, comfort, and assure us in any way that leads to our ultimate growth, then my answer is a resounding yes!"

The difference is important. If we want to use personal revelation to avoid decisions and responsibility, then it conflicts with Heavenly Father's objectives for us. And yet I believe that Father wants to be a partner, a friend, a father who, in the finest tradition of parenting, will lead, bless, and teach his children.

At times I think I have made every mistake in my effort to get guidance from Heavenly Father. The most fundamental may be misunderstanding how to talk with the Father. Virtually every sacrament meeting talk I ever heard on prayer climaxes with an earnest injunction along these lines: We must take time to listen. So, resolved to be a better communicator I go through the thanks and the requests and then I offer him equal time by clearing my mind as I wait for instructions.

But nature hates a vacuum. Soon my empty mind is remembering that I forgot to turn in a report at work, and then I'm fretting about upcoming presentations or household repairs. Of course, I blame my failure on my lack of resolve or lack of character.

But maybe the process is flawed. Inspired by a talk by Stephen Covey, I have learned not to take an empty mind to the Father. Instead I ask stewardship questions in order of priority: "What do I need to do to be closer to the living Christ?" He usually reminds me that he and I need to talk more often. "What do I need to do to be a better family member?" He encourages me to be more kind to my gentle wife. But he has also directed me to specific acts, such as apologizing to Sara for insensitivity. "What do I need to do to be a better Latter-day Saint?" Surprisingly, Heavenly Father's requests in this area tend to be fewer and smaller than the mandates of my overwrought sense of duty. He reminds me to call a troubled ward member, or he gives me ideas for a Sunday lesson. "What do I need to do to be a better employee and community member?" Commonly he gives me clear and simple suggestions.

By asking specific questions, I get specific and helpful answers. When I clear my mind, I get a flood of miscellany.

The bane of my early-adulthood prayers was the multiple-choice test. Filled with the generous desire to do right, I would go to Heavenly Father and ask: "I sure want to do right. Should I do option A or option B?" Blank screen. No answer. So I would become more earnest and more demanding: "I could also add option C. I am willing to do what you ask. Just tell me what to do."

I did a version of the multiple-choice prayer when I was seeking guidance about marrying Nancy. She and I had wavered but now were at a stage of making a decision. So we decided to fast one day and meet that evening for prayer. At the appointed time we met and made our way to the local chapel, where we found a quiet classroom and knelt in prayer. "Shall we marry or not?" Nothing. We persisted. But no answer. Finally I asked Nancy if I might remain behind and wrestle with the Father. She left. I wrestled. And the heavens were as brass over my head. I finally became frustrated and went home. What more could I do? How was I to get an answer?

A few days later I was driving along in downtown Provo when new thoughts entered my mind. I had several times felt a warm and affirming peace about my relationship with Nancy. In addition, we shared common values, I enjoyed her company, and she helped me be my best self. So the question came into my mind: "Is the reason you did not answer my question when I prayed that I already know what to do in my mind and heart?"

Pow! I felt the warmth of heaven as powerfully as any other time in my life. Apparently the Father does not work best in the TV quiz show format. Rather he counsels with us as our friend and father. And he wants us to pay attention to the comments he makes along the way.

A related lesson was taught to some disciples on the road to Emmaus. It was not until after the resurrected Christ had revealed himself to them that they were mindful of the heavenly joy they had felt along the way: "Did not our heart burn within us, while he talked with us by the way?" (Luke 24:32.)

Maybe Heavenly Father speaks to us very often and we do not hear him because we expect his message to come in certain ways. We may have to work for years to recognize the still, small voice. Just as with the wind, we may hear the rustling of leaves or we may feel something on our faces, but we may not sense its direction and purpose without close attention.

Maybe our view of prayer as primarily a periodic ritual is faulty. Maybe it should be more of a continuing dialogue punctuated with kneeling thanks. "Yea, cry unto him for mercy; for he is mighty to save. Yea, humble yourselves, and continue in prayer unto him. Cry unto him when ye are in your fields, yea, over all your flocks. Cry unto him in your houses, yea, over all your household, both morning, mid-day, and evening. Yea, cry unto him against the power of your enemies. Yea, cry unto him against the devil, who is an enemy to all righteousness. Cry unto him over the crops of your fields, that ye may prosper in them. Cry over the flocks of your fields, that they may increase. But this is not all; ye must pour out your souls in your closets, and your secret places, and in your wilderness." (Alma 34:18–26.)

I guess Alma has been telling me all along that prayer is more than an occasional litany. It is the characteristic and continuing devotions of the soul. It is a dialogue between friends. It is the constant acknowledgment of our need for him. It is a heartfelt orientation of gratitude.

My best prayer experiences have come in two ways. Some have come as I am going about my work and I am warmed by a feeling of being blessed. I pause in my work and tread water in the warmth of his goodness. The other way is late at night when I am too tired to sleep and I enter our darkened living room to sit and reflect. It is more like just sitting and enjoying the company of a friend than like a dialogue. I look out at our darkened yard and know that he is present in his grand creation and in my life and in my living room. It brings a peace that passes understanding.

Someday I would like to be able to pray as Jesus, that man who spent all day serving, teaching, healing, and loving—the most exhausting of tasks—and then found quiet places at night, while his disciples slept, to visit with his Father, to fill himself up with divine instruction, to cement his purposes with peace. And having spent much of the night in prayer, he would return to service with the dawn of a new day. Wow. Can any of us say too much of his remarkable resolve? "Therefore, let us glory, yea, we will glory in the Lord; yea, we will rejoice, for our joy is full; yea, we will praise our God forever. Behold, who can glory too much in the Lord? Yea, who can say too much of his great power, and of his mercy, and of his long-suffering towards the children of men? Behold, I say unto you, I cannot say the smallest part which I feel." (Alma 26:16.)

Prayer seems to have less to do with getting answers and more to do with building a relationship. How can we teach this to our children? The most important way we can teach it is by living it ourselves through building a relationship with Heavenly Father and building relationships with them, our dear children. We teach them the power of prayer by continuing to seek the face of God in our own lives.

Joseph taught Brigham Young: "Tell the people to be humble and faithful, and be sure to keep the spirit of the Lord and it will lead them right. Be careful and not turn away the small still voice; it will teach you what to do and where to go; it will yield the fruits of the kingdom. Tell the brethren to keep their hearts open to conviction, so that when the Holy Ghost comes to them, their hearts will be ready to receive it. They can tell the Spirit of the

Lord from all other spirits; it will whisper peace and joy to their souls; it will take malice, hatred, strife and all evil from their hearts; and their whole desire will be to do good, bring forth righteousness and build up the kingdom of God." (Elden J. Watson, *Manuscript History of Brigham Young 1846–1847*, 2 vols. [Salt Lake City: Elden Jay Watson, 1971], 2:529.)

Many of us want to plan our lives for weeks, months, and years. Some of that planning may be good. But maybe we must be willing to take up our meager sack at any time and be willing to go in his service. Maybe we need daily, constant personal revelation in order to know how and where he would have us serve. We may find his guidance not only in clear impressions and warm burnings but also in simple thoughts that invite us to serve.

President Heber C. Kimball is reported to have said that "unless one feels . . . before he finishes his prayer a certain wave of the spirit of God, a certain burning in the center of the self, he can be fairly sure that his prayer is not heard under ordinary circumstances" (paraphrased by Truman D. Madsen, "Twenty Questions," in *Speeches of the Year: Summer Devotional* [Provo, Utah: Brigham Young University Press, 1968], p. 5). That is a very high standard for prayers. It suggests that even as we bless the food we can turn to the Father in earnest gratitude and feel his warming response.

We can bring our deepest yearning to family prayer and seek to hear his voice. In my family, as we have used family prayer as a time to focus our faith we have been warmed. As we have used family prayer as a time to be taught, the Lord has shown us how we can serve and bless those for whom we pray.

The pattern of prayer includes humble and continued seeking, openness to his message, and willingness to follow as he directs. The pattern is best taught in families as we pray for each other and those we serve.

It is a great inheritance to give our children the habit of seeking after the Lord. It will lead them to joyous encounters in this life and in eternity.

Twenty-Five

ENTICED BY JOY:
A DIVINE PATTERN

The test of Christian character should be that a man
is a joy-bearing agent to the world.
—Henry Ward Beecher

In King Benjamin's familiar mandate, the initiative and energy come from God, not from us: "For the natural man is an enemy to God, and has been from the fall of Adam, and will be, forever and ever, unless he *yields to the enticings of the Holy Spirit*" (Mosiah 3:19; emphasis added).

We yield to his Spirit. Likewise, in the Doctrine and Covenants the Lord describes those who inherit the celestial kingdom as "they who are just men made perfect through Jesus the mediator of the new covenant, who wrought out this perfect atonement through the shedding of his own blood" (76:69).

An example of such submission comes to mind. We have a friend who was raised with a knowledge of gospel truths. But in her mid teens she strayed from those teachings. Running around seemed more fun than being good. This led to bad decisions and bad relationships. Eventually she became engaged to a seemingly nice guy who offered love and a promise of a better life. But he was cruel and abused her. She became desperate. She was filled with pain and confusion and had lost her vision of holiness and redemption.

She moved in order to escape the pattern of misery and abuse. In her heart, she felt the invitation to return to God. She attended church and began to study the scriptural messages of redemption. Her mind was reluctant to trust. But the enticings of the Spirit kept pulling her toward Heavenly Father. When she finally opened her heart to him, she was flooded by his love. She was overwhelmed. She rejoiced with Ammon: "Who could have supposed that our God would have been so merciful as to have snatched us from our awful, sinful, and polluted state?" (Alma 26:17.) Filled with joy, she became a beacon to wayward family members and troubled friends. She was filled with compassion, love, joy, and peace. She chose to accept a call to serve a mission. She has blessed many lives.

The story is of a real and specific person. And it follows a familiar pattern. Those who discover their own limitations and turn their lives over to God are filled with him.

Richard H. Cracroft has taught us about divine patterns in his remarkable essay titled "The Pattern of Faith and Jolts of Joy: Spiritual Surprises." He traces his own doubt and rebellion and an invitation by a bishop to test obedience. Caught up in missionary service, he was swept by joy. He discovered "surprises of the Spirit—thrilling road signs on the course to eternal life." As Cracroft describes it, "Our Father will send a spark, a surprise, or a shock of recognition as if to say, 'Here, my child, here is a whiff of truth, a thrill of remembrance, a tangible something to remind you—for a moment—that I'm here.'" (In *A Thoughtful Faith*, comp., Philip L. Barlow [Centerville, Utah: Canon Press, 1986], pp. 295, 299.) We can enjoy a continuing lifetime of guidance, growth, and joyous surprises.

In each of our lives the vital ingredients of people, faith, hope, despair, humility, peace, and love are stirred together in a unique combination. But the pattern is always the same. We learn that living without God is tiresome, pointless, and joyless. In despair we turn to him. And he blasts us with his goodness. Time and again we are surprised that he would reach across eternity to comfort and teach us, his rebellious and proud children. But he does. We learn that the only place to find peace, joy, growth, love, hope, and all the promised rewards is in him.

Sometimes we think that the faults in our family members are too much to bear. But he who bore the terrible weight of all our sins can teach us needed lessons about bearing one another's burdens. He whose name is eternal can teach us about patience. Our Redeemer can teach us about rescuing one another. He knows that we can be blessed by looking beyond the irritations of today to the possibilities of eternity.

Maybe a book on family joy should say more about family processes. But the fact is that family joy is just a special case—a very special case—of joy in general. And joy is about Heavenly Father. If we find Father, we have found joy. If we have found joy, we will be better persons, partners, and parents. We will have family joy.

The process requires patience and determination. We will make many mistakes in the process. But it leads to joy. It leads to him. "Behold, he sendeth an invitation unto all men, for the arms of mercy are extended towards them, and he saith: Repent, and I will receive you. Yea, he saith: Come unto me and ye shall partake of the fruit of the tree of life; yea, ye shall eat and drink of the bread and the waters of life freely." (Alma 5:33–34.)

Family is where Heavenly Father teaches us the greatest lessons. But it is also *what* he teaches us. The great lessons of life and love are often learned in families because that is where we are challenged to be patient, understanding, loving, forgiving, and generous. Families. Earthly families. Church families. Neighborhood families. Human families. Heavenly families. Eternal families. If we learn the lessons well, we as a family may join him in the continuing family business of blessing others through family experiences. We may experience joy and rejoicing known only by God and the godly. We may experience kingdoms, principalities, dominions, and eternities of joy.

That is good news. Joyous news. "Now was not this exceeding joy? Behold, this is joy which none receiveth save it be the truly penitent and humble seeker of happiness." (Alma 27:18.)

He who is the master of joy invites us to a fulness of joy. Maybe fulness of joy is when all the people we have loved and all the experiences we have enjoyed are combined into the eternal present. That is fulness. That is the reward of a perfect Father to his earnest children. "Thou wilt shew me the path of life: in thy presence is fulness of joy; at thy right hand there are pleasures for evermore" (Psalm 16:11).

INDEX